EARLY REVIEWS FOR
THE PARTICIPATION GAME

"Norty Cohen's *The Participation Game* begins with the premise that no one pays you to discover the obvious. Only after you read Cohen's original and stimulating book do you realize what is obvious about favorite brands in 2017: they are embraced by consumers, and embracing comes from participation in the brand experience, not from accepting brand messages that were shouted at you by traditional marketers. Cohen shows why brand messaging is so off the mark today, as too many marketers see consumers as unwilling subjects who need (and fail) to be conquered. Our favorite brands are those with whom we have multiple favorable experiences, and the best marketers are those who engineer the right kinds of experiences. *The Participation Game* stimulates the mind by showing fine examples of participation marketing at its best. The book's infographic format reinforces its key message—marketing today is impressionistic, not linear / logical."

– *Michael Farmer, Author:* Madison Avenue Manslaughter:
An Inside View of Fee-Cutting Clients, Profit-Hungry Owners
and Declining Ad Agencies

"Norty Cohen reveals the secrets of how to earn customer loyalty in today's super-connected world. *The Participation Game* is a must-read for every marketer and explains the remarkable changes in consumer behavior."

– *Margaret Duffy, Ph. D., Executive Director, Novak Leadership Institute, Missouri School of Journalism*

"A thoughtful and valuable resource. A great guide to creating the kind of engagement that is so elusive but also so critical. The research and the extensive library of brand stories are well done."

– Tim Manners, founder Shopperstories.com, former publisher of The Hub

"Most marketing books focus on the WHAT, but what you really need is the HOW, and The Participation Game delivers just that. Using a non-traditional format, Cohen guides you through realistic challenges and offers tangible tactical ideas for how to find resonance with your audience. This book is a fluff free, to-the-point manual that will surely deliver a positive ROI for the time you spend reading it."

– Gina Waldhorn, President, Quirky

"A terrific and compelling must read for marketers. Mr. Cohen unlocks and quantifies the "how to" achieve engagement and attachment with today's consumer in a rapidly changing social landscape. Very impressive."

– Raul G. Marmol, Founding Partner of PLUS Consulting, The EPPA Sangria Co, Former SVP/CMO Bacardi USA

"The first thing marketing-oriented leaders and professionals will discover is just how important the concept of participation is to some of the world's strongest brands. Norty does a masterful job of revealing the power behind participation and offers actionable insights to take your brand to new heights."

– Derrick Daye, Branding Strategy Insider.com

IDEAPRESS
PUBLISHING

Published in the United States by IdeaPress Publishing.

IDEAPRESS PUBLISHING | www.ideapresspublishing.com

All trademarks are the property of their respective companies.

Cover Design by Hilary Clements

Layouts and Type Design by Lauren Knobloch

Editor: Rachel McInnis

Researcher and Editing by Jillian Flores

ISBN: 978-1-940858-29-6   ISBN: 978-1-940858-30-2 (e-book)

PROUDLY PRINTED IN THE UNITED STATES OF AMERICA

By Selby Marketing Associates

SPECIAL SALES

IdeaPress Books are available at a special discount for bulk purchases for sales promotions and premiums, or for use in corporate training programs. Special editions, including personalized covers, custom forewords, corporate imprints and bonus content are also available. For more details, email info@ideapresspublishing.com.

No animals were harmed in the writing, printing or distribution of this book. The trees, unfortunately, were not so lucky.

TABLE OF CONTENTS

PREFACE

When was the last time you talked about a TV ad? Were so excited by a commercial, you forwarded it to a friend? Ripped out a print ad to save for later?

....

Mass media and constant repetition of messaging is a brutal formula that fades fast.

It's the punishment for watching what you want—and yet many advertisers can't break the habit.

Eventually, brands will realize it's not about them.

It's about the consumer and their need for original inspiration to help them change their day, their image and their status.

THE SEARCH FOR HOW AND WHY
CONSUMERS ADOPT BRANDS.

For the last five years, we've interviewed more than 5,000 consumers asking their favorite brands. What we learned was that it wasn't always big advertisers who cross the line to loyalty. In fact, the biggest budgets many times don't buy friends at all.

....

I've had the luxury of doing what I love and pursuing ideas every day as a writer and agency owner for thirty plus years. It got even more interesting when I purchased a former church for my creative/digital agency to live in. The church came with a school.

I didn't want a tenant, I'd been one. So I went over to Washington University and met with the business professors. Together, we developed new entrepreneurial ideas, and we paid grad students to run scenarios. We ended up with a complementary business—a national research agency and focus group facility right there on our campus.

For five years, I had two jobs. I ran around the agency taking care of national clients all day. Then in the evenings, I got to watch the research team execute programs, or more often than not, hit the wall. That happened because no one pays you to discover the obvious. "Find us consumers who truly do these things" was the directive—but it's always easier on paper than in reality.

In the context of research methodology, that means lots of preliminary screens to make sure you have the right person—not just someone who wants to get a stipend for a meaningless opinion.

Our team swung and missed all of the time as we got going. We learned to have consumers read us the label on the product from their shelf before we could confirm them as a user. We asked the same question dozens of ways. But it was a pretty simple formula—answer the question or don't get paid.

Several years ago, we had a similar problem on the agency side. We wanted to convince our clients that our ideas were relevant—but we needed proof.

We called in one of our favorite research partners and said, "We want to understand how and why consumers adopt brands." Within a few weeks, a new methodology was born—and we began executing what would become an annual consumer report about their favorite brands. The top down question was "name your favorite brand." There were three empty white boxes for them to fill in.

We then pulled down the menu and started the deep dive.

What emerged are the building blocks for how connectivity will work in the future. It's built with great ideas that build on each other. As you journey with us through our discovery process, you'll see dozens of examples of what others tried.

The cases inform more questions, and you can compare and contrast from a library of more than 3,000 examples. You'll learn how to access those ideas and build your real-time toolbox.

New connection platforms happen all the time. But the stories of what works will always be how we learn.

....

THE POINT IS NOT TO MIMIC THEM— BUT TO BE INSPIRED.

How does connection happen and why? What works? How can you break down the walls of "you know that we know that you know" we're just marketing?

What happens when consumers produce more relevant and shareable content than brands can ever do?

What's the significance of influencers? Is it just awareness? Which ones work better?

When do consumers cross the line to friendship?

The point is not to mimic them—but to be inspired.

I believe that you are what you do—and if you do great work, you'll get more of it.

TOP 100 LIST 2013-2017*

1	Apple	19	American Eagle	37	Honda
2	Nike	20	Disney	38	Levi
3	Samsung	21	Old Navy	39	Hollister
4	Target	22	Toyota	40	Chick-fil-A
5	Amazon	23	Under Armour	41	Michael Kors
6	Sony	24	Express	42	Frito-Lay
7	Wal-Mart	25	Kohl's	43	Netflix
8	Microsoft	26	LG	44	Gamestop
9	Coke	27	Chevrolet	45	Hershey & BMW
10	Google	28	McDonald's	46	Kroger
11	Adidas	29	Hot Topic	47	Dell
12	Nintendo	30	Macy's	48	Sephora
13	Pepsi	31	Converse	49	HP
14	Starbucks	32	Best Buy	50	Costco
15	Victoria's Secret	33	H&M	51	Chipotle
16	Ford	34	Vans	52	Ralph Lauren
17	Forever 21	35	Dr Pepper	53	Aéropostale
18	Jordan	36	GAP	54	Taco Bell

55	Kellogg	72	Pizza Hut	89	Audi
56	Kraft	73	Banana Republic	90	REI
57	Nissan	74	Subaru	91	Mazda
58	ebay	75	Tesla	92	Carter's
59	Playstation	76	Gucci & Jeep	93	Publix
60	Coach	77	Dove	94	Anhueser Busch & YouTube
61	Verizon	78	J. Crew	95	Urban Decay
62	Mountain Dew	79	Puma	96	Anthropologie
63	Trader Joe's	80	Barnes and Noble	97	Subway
64	Nordstrom	81	Wendy's	98	Johnson & Johnson & PG
65	Asus	82	Nestlé	99	Guess
66	Whole Foods	83	Burger King	100	Ross
67	Rue 21	84	AT&T		
68	Dodge	85	HTC		
69	Bath & Body Works	86	JCPenney		
70	Marvel	87	Monster Energy		
71	Valve	88	Facebook		

*Based on 15,000 Millennial consumer write-in responses (3,000 per year)

#45, #76, #90, #93, & #94 Exact Ties

CHAPTER ONE

PARTICIPATION IS THE
X-FACTOR

Traditional advertising messaging has become an act of indecent exposure. The more you do it, the more desperate you look. For most brands, it doesn't deserve a strong share of the mix, but it's a hard habit to break.

This is a bitter pill for most marketers over the age of 40 to swallow because they learned the old system and understand it.

WHAT IS GENUINE TO CONSUMERS? HOW CAN THEY REALLY LOVE AND TRUST A BRAND? WHAT MAKES THEM WANT TO?

Consider taking the traditional purchase funnel and overlaying the media mix.

Now think back 25 years. Advertisers drove consumers to retail. It is still the dominant medium for fast food, cars, mobile and even some packaged goods. The hope is that once the consumer skips over to loyalty, they can be won over. Get them in store; get them to try it—that will stick.

The media mix is like an ocean liner making a slow turn. And it is wasting valuable time every day.

Rarely can an advertiser get a "genuine" emotional connection with just awareness. Genuine by definition is truthful, sincere, honest, authentic…

And that is the new real challenge for traditional media delivery.

THE MARKETING FUNNEL

DISINGENUOUS

one way communication

AWARENESS
CONSIDERATION
CONVERSION
LOYALTY

GENUINE

two way participation

NOW FAST FORWARD
TO TODAY

Many brands are slow to move along. The traditional side still gets the majority of ad dollars.

By continuing to approach messaging from a traditional, top-down, "here is something you need to know," tone, brands easily step over the line. They maintain their status as advertisers—interrupters—sponsors.

What's the role of advertising? Is it a penalty for seeing the video or TV content you want? Is it negative or positive?

Our methodology dug into this and we asked the question a number of ways. "How do you learn about new brands? How do you connect with your favorite brands?"

· AWARENESS ·
CONSIDERATION
CONVERSION
LOYALTY

1990

TRADITIONAL

TV RADIO

PRINT

POS PR

+

2000

BANNER ADS

+

TODAY

PROGRAMMATIC

GOOGLE ADS

SOCIAL ADS

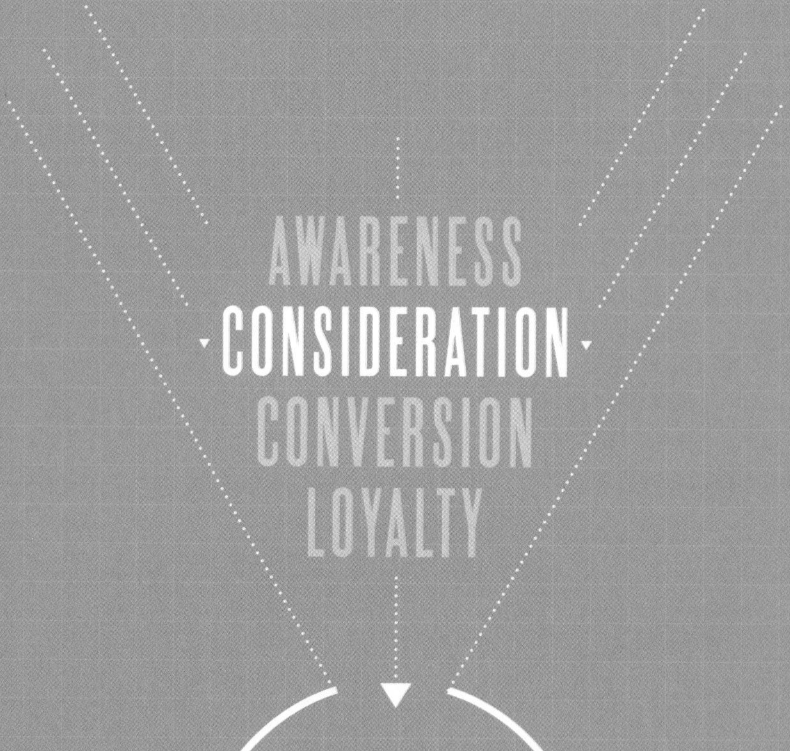

AWARENESS
CONSIDERATION
CONVERSION
LOYALTY

1990

COUPONS | FSI'S |
CONSUMER REPORTS
DIRECT MAIL
MAGAZINES SALES
EXPERIENTIAL/EVENTS PROMOTION
TELEMARKETING

+

2000

WEBSITES **PPC**
SEARCH/SEO
RE-MESSAGING
QR CODES/SNAP TAGS

+

TODAY

BLOGGER
NATIVE ADVERTISING
MOBILE COUPONING LINK BAIT
INFLUENCERS
RE-TARGETING

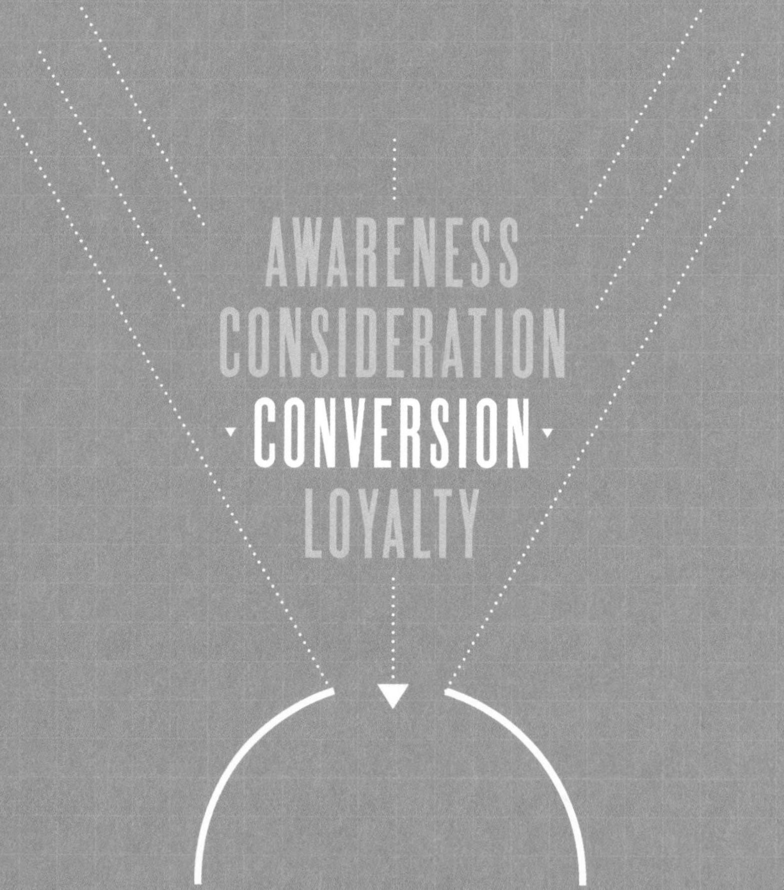

AWARENESS
CONSIDERATION
·CONVERSION·
LOYALTY

1990

IN-STORE

+

2000

SOCIAL CONTENT

YOUTUBE

APPS

ONLINE CONTESTS

+

TODAY

OPT IN

GAMIFICATION

CLICK _to_ BUY

PUSH NOTIFICATION

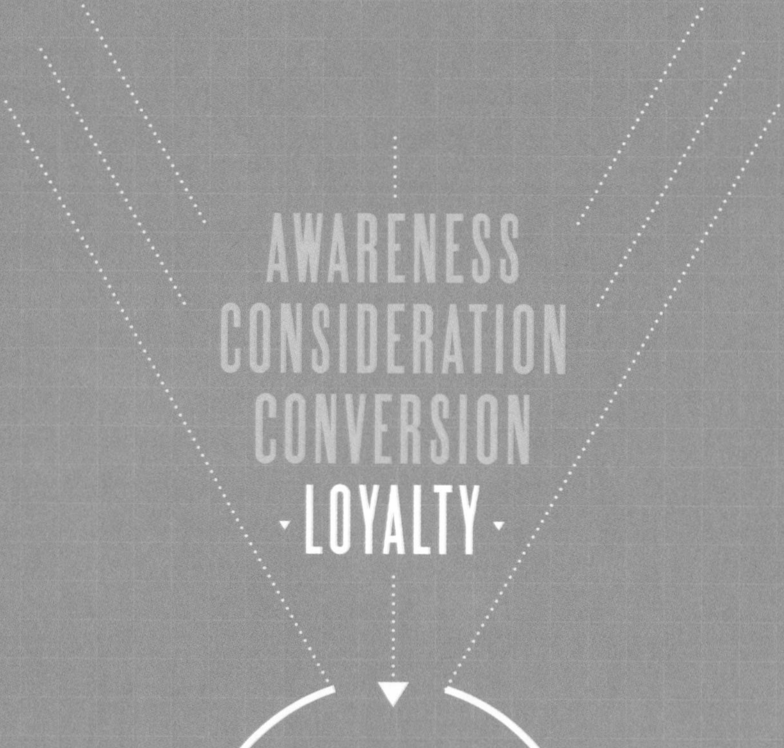

AWARENESS
CONSIDERATION
CONVERSION
· LOYALTY ·

1990

REWARDS

CLUB MEMBERSHIP

SWEEPSTAKES

PERSONALIZED PHONE CALLS

| PUNCH CARDS |

SALES CALLS

GAMES/CONTESTS

+

2000

CRM ECOM

EXPERIENTIAL

+

TODAY

VIDEO

ROBUST CLUB

CO-CREATION

MEMBERSHIPS

IDENTIFYING THE
X FACTOR

Our research chose the most influential early adopters of media—millennial consumers. By definition, they are first generation digital natives born in 1980. We began at ages 13-33 and went to 17-37 years old.

....

They started with three empty boxes and this question: Who are your three favorite brands? This was repeated 5,000 times over five years.

The unaided reveal of their favorite brands led to pull-down menus. With this brand in mind, how do you make decisions?

Looking at the favorites, we interviewed and studied their programming.

what we found was there is an

FACTOR

that can be applied to the media mix:

PARTICIPATION

PARTICIPATION

=

EFFECTIVE RESPONSE

x participation = effective response

It's the purest form of connectivity because it's not about the advertiser.

IT'S ABOUT THE CONSUMER.

As a marketer, can you stop talking about yourself long enough to do that?

HOW WENDY'S PROVED THE
PARTICIPATION GAME

Wendy's has separated itself from other fast food restaurants in a big way over the last five years. They have turned every quadrant into an effective tool by changing the game to participation.

....

Brandon Rhoten, former VP, Head of Advertising, Media and Digital at Wendy's (now at Papa John's), embraced the challenge and was given an opportunity to shake up his category. His team took the medium with the biggest budget and began an approach that set the tone for allowing consumers to share their voice.

The Pretzel Bacon Cheeseburger campaign first aired in 2013 and evolved for several years. Consumers were invited to submit song lyrics using a hashtag. Wendy's then turned those over to campy singers who voiced love songs. These songs aired over dramatic visual enactments of the sentiments, accentuated by a graphic featuring the consumer's original social media post, complete with their name,

"We really didn't leave behind the traditional approach, just decided we didn't need to solely focus on the traditional way in. A great way to make people care is to let them join in on the communication." – Rhoten

handle and profile pic. From there, consumers ran with it. They created their own videos. They were the authors of their own songs. They made spoofs.

"Like any good work, it took on a life of its own quickly. People shared, reporters wanted to talk about it, and we started hearing from internal stake-holders that something felt different about the way we were marketing," Rhoten said.

More importantly, it looked at the one-way communication of TV and turned it on its side. Literally, the message was

WE KNOW THAT YOU KNOW THAT WE KNOW WE'RE JUST TALKING ABOUT A HAMBURGER.

So instead of extolling the values of the product—they let viewers participate in their brand.

They were awarded in spades. Sales and loyalty went up. More variations of the theme came next. They did a series called "Earned It." In this one, consumers just needed to use a hashtag to say what insignificant achievement they had accomplished to deserve a bacon cheeseburger.

"It took over a year before we started seeing serious traction. Which is why many companies become frustrated with branding efforts. It takes time and effort to build a relationship with consumers."

– Rhoten

"Someone doesn't become your friend overnight and certainly not a brand's friend because of one commercial," Rhoten said.

All of this hashtag, and later emoji, connectivity led to more targeted communication through social channels that could be amplified with paid social media. And the X factor was that once Wendy's pioneered the concept of a consumer as star for almost no reason at all, the brand grew its base. Consumers felt good about them.

Granted, they still have to deliver the product well—as does their competition. But advertisers who continue to compete on product attributes and discounting alone are continuing to slip and slide.

"We try to consciously treat every medium like digital marketing now—no dead ends. There's always a link, a phone number, something to lead you down the rabbit hole and hopefully closer to buying the product," Rhoten said.

THE SURPRISING CATEGORY THAT
JUST DOESN'T GET IT

In fact, over a five year period, the top 94 out of 100 brands did not include one beer brand. Their share of spend is constant but their share of market continues to erode.

....

Anheuser-Busch has a marketing brand spend of over half a billion dollars annually. Bud Light and Budweiser ads fill most of this—and they continue to drive new messages and campaigns featuring lifestyle examples of consumers enjoying their products. But exactly the opposite has happened. Their share of spend is constant but their share continues to erode.

There was a time when consumers used beer as a badge. It represented who they were. Bud and Bud Light had formulas of creative, fun ads that would become part of the vernacular.

Super Bowl is the poster child for them. And they flushed more money down the toilet in one game than most brands spend in a year. In 2014, they forgot who their audience was and made fun of them with "Proudly a Macro," a $4 million spot that hissed and treated microbrews like they were Bill Gates in high school.

The spot made fun of "peach pumpkin ale" as a bizarre flavor profile. Consumers were so incensed that they promptly made it the best-selling variety of micros for the year 2015.

Not to mention that Anheuser-Busch not only actually owned the microbrewery that was making peach pumpkin ale, but they were also showing caricatures of hipsters, the very people they were "targeting."

They did get consumer participation. The microbrew community launched an assault based on the trajectory of their attack. They produced a video that got its fair share of views making fun of Anheuser-Busch making fun of them. (Note: in late summer 2016, the Craft Beer Alliance extended a new 10-year marketing agreement.)

CONTINUING TO ENGAGE
IN MARKETING WARFARE
WON'T WORK LONGTERM

Take a look at the mobile telecom industry— it's engaged in high-profile TV marketing warfare.

A few big players are spending above beer levels for awareness of a diminishing margin business. As they push for differentiation, they are counting on the in-store experience to close the sale. They have to count on it. It's an endless cycle—because buying a phone plan is basically a negative experience.

So, like many advertisers, to off-set that negative, they're easily sliding into the quick fix of price promotions. Cars, telecom, fast food and other quadrant one advertisers drive purchase with short-term pricing events.

So what's the

SMARTER ALTERNATIVE

for today's marketplace?

HP RIDES THE WAVE
PIZZA HUT, NOT SO MUCH

"You have to let your brand be part of the culture and bring that culture into the brand," says Vikrant Batra, Global Head of Marketing at HP.

....

HP began an influencer campaign by hiring well-known documentary film-maker Ian Walsh to capture the preparation that surfers use HP laptops for—capturing wave movements and weather tracking. "We wanted to be authentic to their community and create shareable video," he told me.

"We did a documentary that showed how some of the technology available in HP laptops helps big wave professional surfers. We hired Ian Walsh, who was a pro surfer, and Taylor Steele, who was a famous surf filmmaker. It was a very authentic seven-minute documentary that showed what it takes to be a professional surfer."

The crew saw the wave coming and traveled to South Africa where it was about to hit. They drove through the night monitoring it on their HP laptop. They found it in the dead of night. They saw the energy of the swell. With no one around, in an area that had never been surfed, Ian got out there and caught it. And HP caught it on film.

GHOSTWAVE

About the same time, Pizza Hut and Pepsi did a high-budget spot in which another well-known international surfer is shown ordering a pizza from his phone while mastering a wave. The spot then brought in a helicopter to deliver the pizza, with Morgan Freeman narrating.

The result was scathing online chatter about the sell-out:

"Ancient surfers of the South Pacific are turning in their graves."

"Ruining the sport."

"I didn't know there was a Pizza hut in Tahiti."

Both made an attempt to ride a wave and get attention. Consumers could tell the difference.

It's clear that ads like a surfer ordering a pizza on a wave or price promotion wireless deals don't drive loyalty. By definition, it's still not about the consumer. We'll see in future chapters how status is shared by consumers and used as a reason to participate. Price doesn't equate to status. It erodes it. Stunts are cosmetic.

In an unforgiving, real-time environment, everything has to change. As we bend the hanger, let's take a look at how we got there.

THE MILITARY INFLUENCE OF
MARKETING

The military brings us a lot of great things. Discipline, order, tradition and the basic freedoms that we enjoy every day. It also brought us the structure that, until recently, has driven the way marketing was done.

Somewhere along the line in the '50s, advertisers began equating everything about media to military might. The terminology was a perfect fit. No one loved it more than the guys in the C-suites, who had an exclusive relationship between their budgets and their boards.

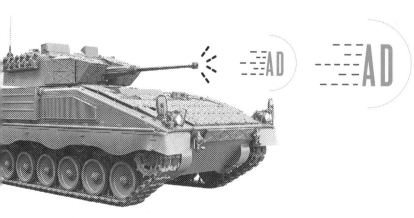

ALL MARKETING PLANS, PAST AND PRESENT, ARE BATTLE PLANS WITH SOME VARIATIONS OF THESE:

STRATEGY UNIT

MISSION STATEMENT

OBJECTIVE

PLANNING
SHORT *and* LONG RANGE

BRIEFING

FLANKERS

ATTACK **FEASIBILITY**

TRACKING

TARGET *TACTICS*

FREQUENCY

TRAFFICKING GUERILLA *BLITZ*

SCALE **EXECUTION**

WEAPONS OF MASS PERSUASION

There was a common acceptance of order from classically trained brand marketers. Al Ries and Jack Trout, two of the most celebrated marketers of the era, published the definitive book Marketing Warfare *in 1986. These were the same guys who defined brand marketing with* Positioning, The Battle for the Mind, *a decade earlier.*

The theories equate military chess games to marketing products and brands.

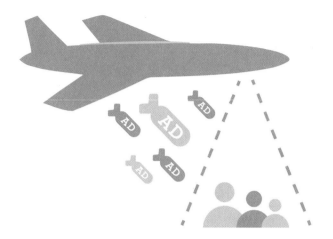

The winner had the most troops, i.e. media budget. Big armies crushed small armies. If you were small you could execute a flanker attack—find a flaw in the big army's business model and hit them when they're not looking.

They used the classic examples that were marketing idioms— Hertz vs Avis or Wendy's vs McDonald's. There was one tool: TV. Hit them hard with on-air copy.

Ries and Trout believed that small companies need to act like big companies and big companies need to act like small companies. They believed that strategy tolerates "run of the mill" tactics.

They laid out an indelible road map. And they gave us a hint to the future. They identified that just like laugh tracks on sitcoms, "people pay more attention to the opinions of others than they do their own." They had a great argument for winning the masses—move them by showing what others are doing. It was the breadcrumb we're still following today.

FROM MAKING WAR
TO MAKING LOVE

The decade of the '80s gave way to expanded thinking about how to win over consumers through emotion. In his ground-breaking book *Lovemarks*, Kevin Roberts set the tone for a number of key principles. The first was the respect/love axis which defined the need to listen to consumers.

Roberts' thesis was that advertising needs to do three things in order to be believable:

MAKE YOU LAUGH, MAKE YOU CRY OR MAKE YOU THINK.

He saw that the mediums would be interactive and articulated the importance of truly being part of a consumer's everyday life. There was meaning in how they interacted that could lovingly be understood and articulated.

Brands
Low Love
High Respect

Lovemarks
High Love
High Respect

LOVE

Products
Low Love
Low Respect

RESPECT

Fads
High Love
Low Respect

PRO TIP

MAKE LOVE

NOT WAR

ENTER A NEW FORM OF
CONSUMER FEEDBACK

The world changed in the midst of Facebook's rise to stardom. Until then, radio call-ins and letters to the editor were the best way to hear from consumers.

This new generation got more of everything—more communication, more rewards and sophisticated video gaming. All of this was shaping how they would interact and setting up a new standard of connectivity.

....

We saw it start to break through in the marketing world with Burger King in 2004. It started with their longstanding message "Have It Your Way," but twisted it a bit for the launch of a chicken sandwich.

HAVE YOU SEEN THIS CHICKEN?

male/big build/brownish features/giant green eyes/red comb and wattles
Known for running in place, doing jumping jacks, and spontaneous dancing on command.
Last seen on subservientchicken.com

If found, please email chicken@burgerking.com

Of course there was a TV spot, but the real energy—
and consumer reaction—was focused on a "viral" website.
Users logged on to see lo-fi, webcam style video of a person
in a chicken costume standing in the middle of a shabby
apartment. A text box invited consumers to "Get chicken
just the way you like it. Type in your command here."

The chicken could respond to more than 300 commands,
ranging from the typical to the weird—the marketing team
predicted the sort of stuff their target might say, and they
prepared for it with pre-recorded clips. Users could play,
and they could share.

And share they did, making it one of the
most viral and buzzworthy efforts of its time.

SUBSERVIENT CHICKEN SET A NEW STANDARD IN TONALITY AND HOW TO RELATE TO CONSUMERS.

It was captivating and took gaming
and playfulness to a new level for brands.

The concept showed an emotional experience could transcend from gaming to "storytelling," and all of it paved the way for more meaningful consumer relationships.

This is what Kobe Fuller, a principal at Accel Partners said about engagement in a 2014 Tech Crunch interview, "Through a story, startups connect through emotion-driven marketing, which creates more authentic moments of customer engagement."

The challenge is now full circle. The principles of military warfare and the awareness of emotional connectivity has everyone doing a lot of the same thing.

IT'S THE NEW PRICE OF ADMISSION:
LOTS OF CONTENT
LOTS OF EMOTION
LOTS OF STORIES
LOTS OF GAMES

HOW DO YOU
BREAK THROUGH
TOMORROW?

So what is the marketing plan of the future? How do brands push through it? Whenever we asked about connections, traditional kept losing the battle.

As consumers told us about their favorite brands, and why and how they were connecting, we heard a different story.

THEY WEREN'T TELLING US ABOUT MESSAGES. THEY WERE TELLING US ABOUT PARTICIPATION.

and this truth emerged:

PEOPLE DON'T
CONSUME ADVERTISING

THEY PARTICIPATE
IN BRANDS

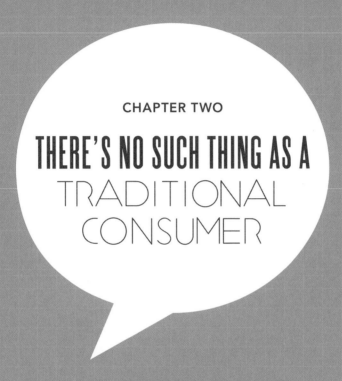

CHAPTER TWO

THERE'S NO SUCH THING AS A TRADITIONAL CONSUMER

In our research, one of the first things we asked consumers was how they discover brands. We phrased it in a number of ways—but it came down to one key principle, the breadcrumb that actually holds true from Ries and Trout—they value the opinions of others first.

The research isolated key consumer groups, both male and female, in five year increments of age. Once they told us their favorite brand, we began the process of drilling down to the how and why.

DISCOVERING
BRANDS AND PRODUCTS

Here's how they answered the question

"HOW DO YOU DISCOVER NEW BRANDS?"

If the purpose of advertising is to bring awareness, it's being sorely outplayed by consumer conversations. Clearly, to push any new information into the mainstream, awareness has a much easier chance if you give consumers something to talk about.

What other people have to say is at minimum four times more effective than advertising.

AWARENESS

has a much easier chance if you

GIVE CONSUMERS SOMETHING TO TALK ABOUT

HOW THEY DISCOVER BRANDS

Digital is key in brand discovery

FRIENDS OR FAMILY

83%

♂	♀	ıl	ıl
78%	87%	80%	84%

INFLUENCER POSTS

52%

♂	♀	ıl	ıl
47%	58%	53%	52%

ONLINE WORD OF MOUTH

39%

♂	♀	ıl	ıl
36%	42%	34%	41%

FACEBOOK ADS

28%

♂	♀	ıl	ıl
21%	34%	28%	28%

TV ADS

26%

♂	♀	ıl	ıl
25%	28%	29%	25%

WEB SEARCH (NON PAID)

20%

♂	♀	ıl	ıl
19%	22%	20%	wq%

MALE ♂ 16-36 .... FEMALE ♀ 16-36 ....

WRITTEN REVIEWS

35%

♂	♀	ıl	ıl
32%	38%	32%	36%

SEE AND TOUCH

34%

♂	♀	ıl	ıl
27%	42%	34%	35%

BRAND'S SOCIAL POSTS

31%

♂	♀	ıl	ıl
28%	35%	29%	32%

NEWS STORIES

20%

♂	♀	ıl	ıl
18%	21%	17%	21%

YOUTUBE ADS

18%

♂	♀	ıl	ıl
21%	14%	29%	14%

EMAIL NEWSLETTERS

16%

♂	♀	ıl	ıl
14%	18%	19%	14%

YOUNG ı| 16-26   OLD ı| 27-36

NOBODY WANTS TO CONSUME
TRADITIONAL MARKETING

Next follow up question—what do you need to know before you make a purchase? In this list, respondents were given 24 ways they could learn about new products.

···

The top four were again dominated by what other people are saying. Anyone. Bloggers, influencers—even paid posts. Advertising is relegated to the bottom of the list. It has been tainted by lack of endorsement and an air of desperation. Being discovered is cool. Trying too hard isn't.

We've gone through a period where advertisers are still making their :30 spot the hero—then looking for its appearance in other mediums. Most are learning that each medium requires its own vernacular and "in-the-know" style. But there's really no reason to convert a TV idea—particularly when only ⅓ of consumers are watching live TV.

$ BEFORE I BUY

Word of mouth is irreplaceable, but online is where influence takes place.

1 WOM from Friends/Family

2 WOM from Online Posts

3 Product Reviews

4 Posts Featuring Brands

5 Blogs

6 Company Posts

7 Brand Emails

8 Facebook Ads

9 News Stories

10 Video Reviews

11 YouTube Ads

12 Blogs by Brand Advocates

13 Branded Email Newsletters

14 User Created Video How-To Guides

15 Non-Paid Web-Search Results

16 Twitter Ads

17 TV Ads

18 Branded How-To Guides

19 Printed Ads

20 Paid Video Advertisements

21 Paid Endorsements

22 Celebrity Influencer Posts

23 Radio Ads

24 Paid Ads Web Search

Respondents ranked their top 5 out of 24 responses

....

GIVING THEM SOMETHING TO TALK ABOUT

TAKE 5 SWAG EXCHANGE

Recently, Hershey's was looking to re-launch their Take5 candy bar, so awareness would be a top goal. Historically, that would mean traditional advertising. Instead, they developed a concept called "swag exchange" and brought it to a highly connected audience at SXSW.

They knew that SXSW attendees were receiving a lot of merchandise, so they created an intuitive bartering system. Bring us something you don't want, and we'll give you something you want, or—even better—need. Those things ranged from ponchos on rainy days to reservations at exclusive restaurants to tech gadgets, and a few branded items as well. They calculated the value of the swag like a stock exchange (hence, "swag exchange"), based on supply and demand, with a very SXSW-worthy algorithm.

How did it relate to Take5? Well, they positioned the relaunch of the candy bar as a remix and declared they were "remixing" the swag experience. But truly, they found a real consumer problem (too much free stuff they didn't really want) and solved it in a meaningful and fun way. So this unexpected surprise and delight turned into a couple of hundred million impressions. This is giving them something to talk about.

MCDONALD'S PAY WITH LOVING

McDonald's took their "I'm Lovin' It" campaign to breakthrough connectivity with their "Pay with Loving" concept. Cashiers invited a random sampling of consumers to execute a random "Act of Lovin'" as payment for their order—which could include high fives, making someone smile, calling a loved one, or anything else they deemed fit within the theme.

They were then encouraged to tell the world about it and a new level of interest was born for their brand. McDonald's felt good enough about the idea to use it as their Super Bowl commercial. Participants were chosen randomly—for this to work it didn't always have to reward consumers—just enough to get into the conversation stream.

KATE SPADE #MISSADVENTURE

Kate Spade broke the mold when they decided to forego the traditional :30 spot with a combination of entertainment and relatable fun.

The "#missadventure" series is now in its second season. Stars like Anna Kendrick, Zosia Mamet and influential others ham it up for the camera and find themselves in everyday situations. The stories are scripted, humorous and, above all, entertaining. The props are all quite naturally Kate Spade items—and the videos are bite sized enough to share.

It's a pretty simple formula that also ties into a retail component for immediate shopping. Sharing plus shopping. Intuition. And not looking like an advertiser.

CAPTAIN AMERICA: CIVIL WAR TWITTER EMOJIS

When Marvel was ready to launch the movie *Captain America: Civil War*, they wanted to mobilize its consumer troops. They decided to use Twitter as their medium and introduced two hashtags: #TeamCap and #TeamIronMan—and directed their fans to pick sides and build their teams.

When fans used the character-specific hashtags (which corresponded with one side or the other, of course) their Tweet populated with the character's emoji. Those who used the hashtags earned the chance to win a non-speaking, walk-on part in the next Avenger's movie.

Having fun. Playing along. Giving them something to talk about (and, in the case of the emojis, talk with).

SAY IT WITH PEPSI CANS

Pepsi took the expressive idea of emojis in a different direction—they actually put a series of 200 of them on their package. Giving a Pepsi became not just a drink, but an expression of thought.

Providing consumers an opportunity to play with the brand on a universal level—i.e, the whole world, across markets—takes a really simple formula. Find the can, give it to someone and you have participated. Or with a simple download, you can use the "Say It with Pepsi" emoji keyboard on your mobile device. It works.

But even better, they brought the idea to partners like Pizza Hut. Consumers who "find" bottles with pizza emojis can trade them in for free pizzas.

Simplicity as a formula continues to evolve.

MOUNTAIN DEW
DEWCISION 2016

Mountain Dew turned the idea of a brand launch on its head with an idea that didn't center on traditional. Mountain Dew users have a special relationship with their brand— and the brand found a way to harness their voice and get people talking.

Only so many flavors can fit on a shelf—so why not let consumers decide which ones get the slot. They created DEWcision 2016 and played into the most talked-about topic of the year: the presidential election. Both potential flavors featured a hashtag and were accented by video stunts and VR executions featuring entertaining competitions.

GAMING.
PARTICIPATION.
ENTERTAINMENT.

*And people discovering
a brand's new product
through the resulting talk.*

PUT THE IDEAS INTO
PLAY

*It's clear the era of traditional advertising reigning
supreme is over. But how do you transition your business
and long-held marketing techniques? Try this thought
starter exercise to get thinking differently.*

THOUGHT STARTER EXERCISE

Objective:
Break away from traditional strategies for brand discovery.

Participation Game Strategy:
We now know that 83% of consumers turn to word of mouth (friends and family) to learn about new brands. So the key is evangelizing your audience to create greater awareness of your brand.

Thought Starters:
How can you insert yourself into a current ongoing conversation? Think about:

- *Experiences they will be having (i.e. Hershey's knew the Take5 target would be at SXSW.)*

- *Where they are already going for conversation (i.e. Kate Spade leveraged celebrities their target loved.)*

How can you enhance the way they are having conversations? (i.e. Marvel and Pepsi both knew consumers talk to each other through emojis so they gave them a new way to share emojis).

Notes:
....
....
....
....
....
....
....
....
....
....
....
....
....
....
....
....
....
....
....
....
....
....

Notes:

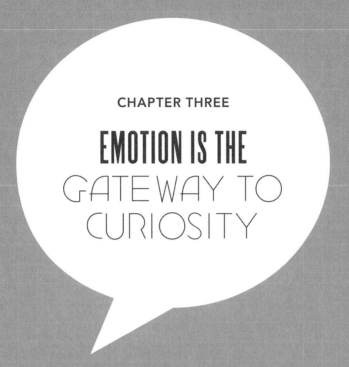

CHAPTER THREE

EMOTION IS THE
GATEWAY TO
CURIOSITY

As we continued to find benchmarks to measure the dynamics of brand loyalty, we discovered Robert Plutchik's Wheel of Emotion. Much like a color wheel, it shows the relationships between emotions—which of them are polar opposites, which are related and how the emotion changes with intensity (for instance, boredom is a derivative of the core emotion of loathing).

As a brand marketer, studying the wheel and deciding how to utilize emotion to anchor your message can be unifying for all parties.

START WITH FEELINGS
NOT ATTRIBUTES

Again, you've stepped away from topline messaging. Leave it aside for now. Yes, you need to tell people about the relevant seasonality and product attributes—and you will, once you have piqued their curiosity and earned their attention with emotion. Ultimately, the adage applies:

NO ONE CARES HOW MUCH YOU KNOW, TILL THEY KNOW HOW MUCH YOU CARE.

Kevin Robert's thesis was that emotion tops all—that consumers connect first emotionally and that it's possible for brands to live in this zone. The approach was to start with a love relationship—then move onto messaging and distribution.

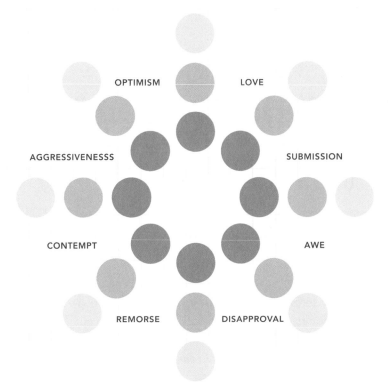

OPTIMISM

LOVE

AGGRESSIVENESSS

SUBMISSION

CONTEMPT

AWE

REMORSE

DISAPPROVAL

*Robert Plutchik's,
Wheel of Emotion*

*Much like a color wheel,
it shows the*

RELATIONSHIPS BETWEEN EMOTIONS

*which of them are polar
opposites, which are related
and how the emotion changes
with intensity.*

EMOTIONS IN THE AGE
OF CONNECTIVITY

Flash forward to 2013: *Harvard Business Review* published a scientific approach to leveraging emotional connectivity, submitted by Kelsey Libert and Kristin Tynski, from the agency Fractl. They knew on-going and serial content distribution creates a base of SEO and helps to maintain and grow existing large audiences. But also, that viral content could spark growth among smaller audiences and stimulate engagement. They set out to understand the powerful role of emotion in marketing campaigns that successfully go viral.

They looked at top images from image sharing sites (imgur.com and Reddit) and surveyed consumers on their emotional responses to each image, plotting them on Plutchik's wheel.

....

For these, the most shared and distributed content, the emotions that fit into the surprise and anticipation segments of the wheel were overwhelmingly represented. Specifically, curiosity, amazement, interest, astonishment and uncertainty. Highly shared content seemed to favor admiration.

HIGHLY SHARED CONTENT

·····································

seemed to favor

·····································

ADMIRATION

so what does that mean for your brand?

JOY, TRUST AND ANTICIPATION

Once we read the *Harvard Business Review* report, we took the entire wheel and shared it with 5,000 consumers over a five-year span and asked them to help us understand which emotions connect them to their favorite brands.

The question immediately following the naming of their favorite three brands was, "What emotion has your favorite brand caused you to have in the last 30 days?"

....

The clear winner each time was joy, then trust, then anticipation and surprise. Interestingly, it holds true for each of their top three favorite brands almost identically. People's top three brands bring them joy first and foremost, then trust and anticipation, with surprise rounding out the fourth spot across the board.

*My top three
brands bring me*

JOY FIRST
AND FOREMOST

*then trust and
anticipation.*

BRANDS HAVE FEELINGS, TOO

Top brands keep millennials warm and fuzzy

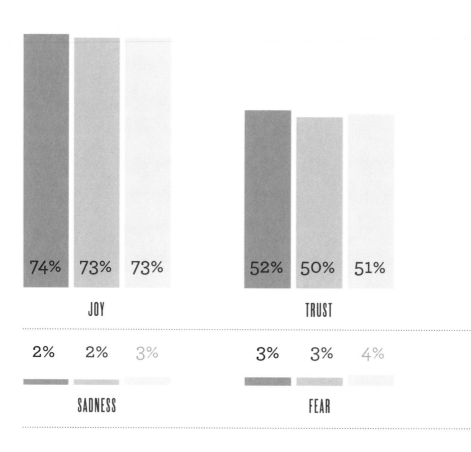

| 74% | 73% | 73% |
| JOY |

| 52% | 50% | 51% |
| TRUST |

| 2% | 2% | 3% |
| SADNESS |

| 3% | 3% | 4% |
| FEAR |

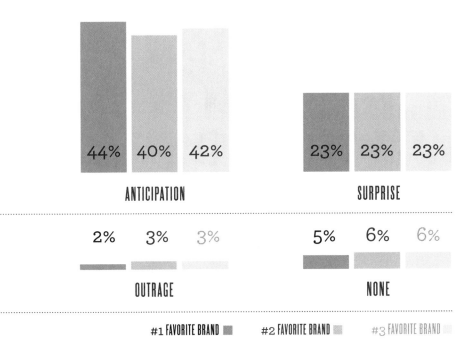

ANTICIPATION 44% 40% 42%

SURPRISE 23% 23% 23%

OUTRAGE 2% 3% 3%

NONE 5% 6% 6%

#1 FAVORITE BRAND #2 FAVORITE BRAND #3 FAVORITE BRAND

BRINGING EMOTION
TO YOUR BRAND

So when you're building a product, a purpose—and ultimately a profit plan—for a brand, this is saying,

"LOOK, YOUR MISSION NEEDS TO BE TO CREATE JOY FOR CONSUMERS. HOW CAN YOU DESIGN YOUR EXPERIENCE TO DO THAT?"

So let's say you're in the telecom industry, which we've already established currently focuses on price wars for differentiation. How can a visit to the phone store be joyful?

All of the conversations about honesty and genuine sincerity are played out when they've chosen trust almost evenly across the board. What's the benchmark for trust? Eighty-three percent of online respondents in 60 countries say they trust the recommendations of friends and family, according to a recent Nielsen Global Trust in Advertising report.

So building trust is also the
BRIDGE TO WORD OF MOUTH.

Where does anticipation fit in their daily lives? It's easy to see how you can build anticipation around a new product launch, but how do you become the brand that continually tells consumers, "good stuff is coming"? Clearly consumers value it—and as obtuse as the word is—they chose it third each time.

Perhaps your brand can't be all three. But if you want to be in their top three—or act like a brand in their top three, at least—pick one and do it well.

see it in action

....

DRIVING GENUINE
EMOTIONAL RESPONSE

COCA-COLA #COKEMYNAME

Coca-Cola works extremely hard to tread in the world of emotion—and they've maintained their four-year status among the top 100 brands in our studies. The formula: stop talking about yourself and talk about consumers.

As they individualized cans and bottles with first names as part of their "Share a Coke," campaign, they went even further with a billboard in Times Square. Fans who tweeted #Cokemyname could fire off a tweet and see a digital message on the billboard with fun facts about their name within two minutes.

It was all powered by a microsite that stored the most popular names. A webcam across the street automatically snapped a picture of the person's name and they received re-tweetable content back.

Joy, anticipation and surprise—all in one nice little package.

STARBUCKS TWEET A COFFEE AND COCA-COLA SHARE A COKE

The logical and most tactile extension of generating joy was framed similarly by both Starbucks and Coca-Cola.

"Tweet A Coffee" linked the technology of that moment into real time. Starbucks cardholders could send a $5 gift card to a friend by puting both @tweetacoffee and their friend's Twitter handle in a tweet (as long as they'd linked their Starbucks card account to Twitter, of course).

Coca-Cola put even more behind the idea with Share A Coke—and found even more extensions and promotion by linking it to Regal Cinemas. Once users entered their credit card information, they were able to send a Coke simply by tweeting at @TweetaCoke. Users received a virtual gift card for $5, redeemable at any Regal Cinemas, to tweet to a friend.

The formula of sharing joy was easy at that point. It's both the joy of giving and of receiving, and these brands made it happen without getting in the way. After all, doesn't a small gift from a friend generate more joy than a low-value freebie from a brand?

HONDA DREAM TRACK

Any time you can ask a consumer for an opinion, the more trust you can build. But you have to use it and show them you're listening.

Honda decided to ask its friends to help design a racetrack for the new Civic coupe. With social media distribution on Facebook and Twitter, the communication simply asked for ideas for the "Dream Track." Consumers saw the opportunity to let loose, providing details for brand-generated ideas (like what a giant piñata should look like and be filled with), but also submitting ideas for stunts of their own imagining.

Ideas that got used were rewarded with a personal shout out to the user who submitted it. While the final result was debuted with a video shared across all social channels, users got sneak peek previews on Snapchat.

Asking for opinions, actually using them and saying thank you with shout outs—all drives trust. Throw in some playful fun for extra measure, and you cover off on joy and surprise, too.

STARBUCKS FLAVOFF

Starbucks originated a really simple idea that pulls all of the consumer levers with an overlay on a promotion they would have done anyway. To promote their many flavors of Frappuccino, they simply asked consumers to vote for their favorite on Facebook. Simple, geo-targeted, paid and effective, it aggregated their opinions—and luckily for the consumers—offered a special price on the winner. Consumers could turn their favorite flavor into a badge with gifs; further participation led to additional rewards.

Let's be honest. Does Starbucks really care which they say? Their sales already tell them what's popular. But just for fun, let's pretend. Starbucks knows their consumers' orders are a very personal thing, and they're celebrating that and elevating the role that consumers play in the whole transactional experience. And they earned trust for it.

AMERICAN EAGLE #AERIEREAL

Want to build trust? Consider what American Eagle has been able to do—creating a movement and a concept for consumers to participate. Their sub-brand of lingerie, Aerie, recently started using the hashtag #AerieReal—to connote the trend of female empowerment and body positivity. Its tagline, "The Real You is Sexy," began in 2014, when the brand stopped using Photoshop on models.

They then took to Instagram and Twitter to encourage consumers to post real/untouched photos of themselves using the hashtag. For every post, they made a one-dollar donation to the National Eating Disorders Association (NEDA). This then pre-qualifies consumers to be featured on the brand website which showcases "imperfection."

The program has been so successful to date that its media impressions were in the billions and the brand's sales skyrocketed. The brand was willing to support a cause that was meaningful to their consumers, laying the groundwork for trust. Then they generated joy by putting consumers in the spotlight.

A lot of trust with a little joy mixed in makes a powerful cocktail. Consider the value proposition of each post and its influence throughout the poster's network. Then the next time you have $100,000, work backwards. What could you do with a dollar per post?

#AERIEREAL STARTED AS A SPARK
AND HAS IGNITED A MOVEMENT.
IT'S NOT ALL ABOUT FLAWS OR CURVES,
IT'S WHAT'S BENEATH THE SKIN.
#AERIEREAL IS ABOUT LOVING THE REAL YOU.
#AERIEREAL IS ABOUT EMPOWERMENT.

SHARE *YOUR*
SPARK!

#*aerie*REAL

A lot of trust with a little joy mixed in
MAKES A POWERFUL COCKTAIL.

A TASTE OF ALDI

When we saw Walmart show up as favorite brand in our surveys—originally we were shocked. We couldn't get why they were cool. Then it hit us—they are consistent with great products and great prices, which builds trust. So it was not a shock to see the discount grocer ALDI show up on consumers' minds.

They used the element of surprise to change perception about quality, convincing consumers you can purchase gourmet meal ingredients at Aldi. They hired a gourmet chef, enlisted the support of *Bon Appétit* and filmed a dinner party. Ten California foodies were taken to a high-end winery and served a fabulous dinner. They then were challenged to identify which ingredients were from Aldi. The host not only revealed that all the ingredients were from Aldi, but she also underscored it with the incredibly low price per head (less than $15) that the entire meal cost.

Voila, suddenly Aldi is cool. *Bon Appétit* not only created reach for the video and published the recipes for consumers to create at home, but they also lent equity among a discerning crowd. The dinner itself demonstrates the joy of a delicious meal and shared time together, but overall the concept delivers on surprise with an unexpected reveal and trust with endorsement by real foodies.

LAY'S ONE MILLION SUMMER MOMENTS

Instagram is for sharing your favorite photos. Favorite photos = favorite moments. Favorite moments = joy. Lay's did the math here by allowing 200,000 consumers to put their favorite Instagram photo on an actual bag of chips. The program ramped up for two years and helped support the summer selling season.

Consumers could simply go online to build their custom bag (for free). After linking their Instagram account, they were able to then pick a favorite Instagram photo and which Lay's flavor to place it on. Once the actual bag was shipped, social sharing ensued. That's 200,000 posts to 200,000 different feeds when those bags arrive—and that's a lot of endorsers for the cost of a special printing for each bag.

What's more joyful than a brand that celebrates your favorite content by putting it on their product just for you?

PUT THE IDEAS INTO
PLAY

*Throw a little joy, trust and anticipation with a dash
of suprise into your budget. Robert Plutchik laid the
wheel out there for us to overlay onto our programming—
the opportunity is there to build a plan around it.*

THOUGHT STARTER EXERCISE

Objective:

Foster a relationship by sparking genuine emotional responses to your brand activities.

Participation Game Strategy:

Now that we've uncovered that it is crucial for brands to leverage joy, trust and anticipation, let's connect with consumers emotionally first and foremost.

Thought Starters:

How can you create emotion by talking about your consumer, instead of yourself? Think about:

- *Enabling consumers to be the ones to 'take credit' for providing joy (i.e. Starbucks and Coke both acted as the the inspiration for people to give through their 'tweet' activations.)*

- *Opportunities that create a consumer desire to take part in brand conversation (i.e. Honda asked their audience for input and Aerie helped their audience support a movement they already cared about.)*

How can your brand show it cares?

Notes:

....
....
....
....
....
....
....
....
....
....
....
....
....
....
....
....
....
....
....
....
....
....
....
....
....

Notes:

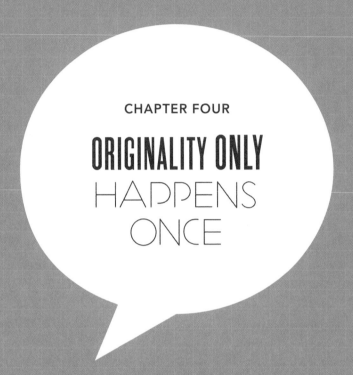

CHAPTER FOUR

ORIGINALITY ONLY HAPPENS ONCE

Consumers are pretty good at knowing when they have an original idea to share. Or if they can get credit for being the first to share yours. But either way, their level of discernment grows more every day.

FIRST THINGS FIRST:
EARN THEIR ATTENTION

When I'm in a room with a group, I love to ask about the last time they put up a post and took it down. Then I ask why. The answer is always something like, "I was politically incorrect." Or, "I didn't look good in the photo." Or, "My friends didn't think it was funny." Finally—the cold hard truth usually comes out when someone says, "Only a few people liked my post." So that's the filter.

Consumers know a good idea from a bad one. They know an original idea from a me-too. And there are more new ones coming out every day. So just like you need to go to the gym, you need to study ideas to keep your creativity in shape.

....

We've been collecting original ideas and documenting them in case study format—broken down by category—since 2008. Readers of this book can access the library with this URL: www.theparticipationgame.com/tracker

UNLOCK YOUR ACCESS
to 3,000 ideas and counting

GO TO
www.theparticipationgame.com/tracker

TO GAIN ACCESS TO MY EVER-GROWING LIBRARY OF BITE-SIZE INDUSTRY REPORTS SO YOU CAN KEEP AN EYE ON WHAT'S BEEN DONE, WHAT'S WORKING AND HOW THINGS ARE CHANGING.

As you develop new ideas for your brand, there is one key that unlocks consumer interest:

PERMISSION

You need an idea good enough to get permission from the consumer to engage with you. There are 3,000 ideas in our database—each no more than a paragraph long. Take ten and work backwards—what made it work? Forget tactics and think ideas.

Consumers are coming up with their own ideas and conducting their own tests on what earns attention by posting an average of 11 pieces of content a day. At the same rate, schools have churned out "mass communication" majors who have client-side jobs. They read about executions other brands are doing. The gig economy provides them with freelancers. The recipe: we need a tactic.

You do not need a tactic. You need an idea. Totally different. Almost impossible to understand for those in the world of cubicles. And tough for freelancers to deliver when they're given a narrow, executional task.

In Adam Grant's book *Originals*, he mentions the site Upworthy and their philosophy on how to write a headline that has the potential to go viral. Their goal is to generate 25 headlines. According to him, "#24 will suck. Then #25 will be a gift from the headline gods and will make you a legend."

So the time to get ideas right is way before you think about tactics. It's not taught that way and certainly not absorbed. But you need a worthy idea in order to earn the permission to connect.

YOU NEED A WORTHY IDEA IN ORDER TO EARN THE PERMISSION TO CONNECT.

NEXT, FIND THE
RIGHT WAY TO CONNECT

Once you've papered the room with raw ideas, working backwards from as many angles as you can, it's time to think about a connection platform.

The ad techs and social media channels are absolutely throwing new dust into marketers' eyes every day. They (and their investors) believe they are monetizing by connecting with brands. A connection platform is a way to deliver an idea; it is not an idea (even if it is a new idea for a new connection platform).

Take for instance the tech vendor Snaps. They make a great emoji keyboard that can facilitate content sharing —and with a download, you even get a direct line to the consumer. But it's not an idea in itself—it's the execution that may or may not be meaningful enough to garner permission. Taco Bell used them to send a taco emoji

*A connection platform is
a way to deliver an idea;
it is not an idea.*

as a moody text that spices things up. So did Burger King, but with chicken fingers. At some point, it's the same idea. Sorry.

For a killer connection platform example, let's look at what McNeil did with Zyrtec's Allergy Cast app. Their insight was based on the insatiable need for allergy sufferers to share how they feel. This app allows users to get up to the minute allergy counts by location, with lots of opt-ins for alerts. It then aggregates the comments that other users are feeling and everyone's opinion is heard. The idea—find a way to make allergy sufferers feel supported. The connection platform—an app—and it is perfectly executed.

When we heard about it, they actually had plans to take it a step further and white label it for Walgreens, allowing the retailer to brand the app as their own. There were coupons involved in the end, of course.

So if you want to move from permission to connection platform, start with ideas. Volumetrically—think of 25 times the number of ideas to connection platforms.

REACH THE PEAK WITH TWO-WAY
COMMUNICATION

If you've nailed down an original idea that gets you permission, and picked the right connection platform, then it's time to graduate from high school. Those are the basics.

Nothing else counts, until you get to two-way communication: creating conversations between brands and people.

....

The Zyrtec Allergy Cast app works because it creates two-way participation. They want to know what the consumer is feeling. The app asks them to log in every day. And they have lots of reasons and coupons to get you back to normal—if you check the box on heavy allergies.

TWO-WAY PARTICIPATION

user-generated content

CONNECTION PLATFORM

begin a dialogue with consumers

PERMISSION

creative, digital and experiential programs

THE NEW
CURRENCY

Howard Tullman is the CEO of 1871, the massive start-up incubator with 300 new concepts brewing all the time in Chicago's Merchandise Mart. He is constantly culling through what's next and coined the phrase "attention is the new currency."

If that's the case, and we know it's about two-way communication, then here's how we look at it. Why spend all your time trying to get attention? Why not give attention? Once you've got a good idea, and you have an established platform for connecting, why not re-allocate the budget for outbound connectivity?

Recent studies show how limited this opportunity can be—so you need plenty of it to capitalize on those precious chances. The average attention span has dropped four seconds since 2000—which could easily be attributed to social and digital smartphone activities.

THE NEW CURRENCY

you can

GET ATTENTION

OR

you can

GIVE ATTENTION

Q: HAVE YOU EVER HAD A TRULY GREAT INTERACTION WITH A BRAND OR COMPANY?

When we asked 1,000 consumers if they've ever had a meaningful two-way interaction with a brand, 16% (or 160 consumers) gave us verbatims. What did they consider to be meaningful? Well, just about everything.

Here's a Few Examples:

Netflix *customer service is always super helpful and sometimes more entertaining than shows on Netflix.*

Nike *customer service fixed something even though the product was out of warranty.*

Nintendo *gave me $70 off because I asked.*

Chipotle *has a team of people that interact with their consumers on social media. Any time I post on Twitter about their product I get retweeted.*

I once tweeted a picture of my **SiriusXM** *in my car showing the song "Gettin' Jiggy Wit It" by Will Smith and included @SiriusXM in it.*

Taco Bell *gave me free drinks because my friends were thirsty.*

The best and most helpful interaction was with my laptop's manufacturer **Acer.** *Their customer service is awesome.*

the average

ATTENTION SPAN OF A

GOLDFISH

9
SECONDS

HUMAN

8
SECONDS

The average attention span
2000: 12 seconds | 2013: 8 seconds

Source : Brain, Attention Span Statistics , January 2014

The takeaway: everything counts. There's a guy driving down the road, sees "Getting Jiggy with It" playing on his Sirius radio. He takes a photo of his dashboard —tweets it with @siriusxm and they re-tweet him. He mentions it as a "meaningful interaction."

There's another person who says, "I get a shout out every now and then." Or the simple idea that they went to the store and someone was nice to them. Think about that. My favorite brand asked me how I was doing. It is just not hard to do.

Twitter has become a customer service hotline, and instead of prescribing tactics, marketers would do well to make sure they are staffing that opportunity every day.

Is it just about customer service though? Not necessarily. The whole concept of Corporate Social Responsibility is valued in the purchase funnel. A report in *Huffington Post* said that nine in 10 consumers would switch brands to a company they believe is doing cause marketing.

And that's just the tip of the iceberg. The idea here is to think about ways you can reflect the attention back to your consumer rather than talking about yourself. Caring is a good look.

The idea here is to

THINK ABOUT WAYS YOU CAN REFLECT THE ATTENTION BACK TO YOUR CONSUMER RATHER THAN TALKING ABOUT YOURSELF.

Caring is a good look.

REALNESS IS A THING

eMarketer published a report that said, "The other component that differentiates online content is realness."

"Marketing used to be smoke and mirrors. It used to be 'go and buy this thing because it's wonderful,' but now everyone can instantly determine whether you're lying about a product based on reviews.

....

"Smartphones have dramatically changed the landscape of advertising. Television hasn't quite caught up. Online, people can talk back. This forces brands to be real and genuine and most brands are terrible at it."

So the lesson here: start with an original idea. Earn the attention of your audience, connect through the right channel and return the attention with two-way interactions. But through it all, you've got to keep it real. Today's consumers can tell the difference.

MY SOCIAL FEED

When deciding where to allow a brand into their social media feed

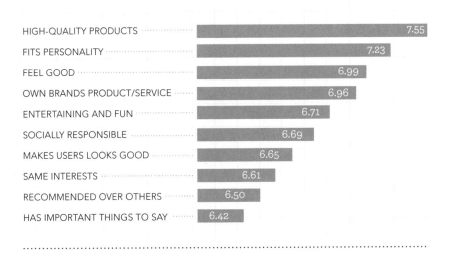

HIGH-QUALITY PRODUCTS	7.55
FITS PERSONALITY	7.23
FEEL GOOD	6.99
OWN BRANDS PRODUCT/SERVICE	6.96
ENTERTAINING AND FUN	6.71
SOCIALLY RESPONSIBLE	6.69
MAKES USERS LOOKS GOOD	6.65
SAME INTERESTS	6.61
RECOMMENDED OVER OTHERS	6.50
HAS IMPORTANT THINGS TO SAY	6.42

Respondents rated on a scale of 1–10

through it all,

YOU'VE GOT TO KEEP IT REAL

*today's consumers can
tell the difference*

let's look at a few brands that are doing it right ⋯⋯⋯▸

WENDY'S #SHARE4ADOPTION

Wendy's took the opportunity to enlist its customers to physically participate in a charity program with their special #Share4Adoption program that benefits the Dave Thomas Foundation. Cups were printed with the call to action and an illustrated hand making half a heart. When the consumer posts a photo of themselves completing the heart using the hashtag, Wendy's made a $5 donation.

The cause—adoption—provided the sense of realness. Not only has Wendy's been associated with adoption for a long time, but their founder Dave Thomas was adopted himself. That's a genuine, believable link and a kid-focused cause consumers could care about. The connection platform was a number of social platforms, and the mechanism for two-way participation was simple and fun.

The program is in its second year of accomplishing a significant $500,000 donation. That means they've achieved at least 100,000 participants. Not too shabby.

We asked our 1,000 consumers, "What does a brand need to do to get into your social feed?" You can see that this Wendy's program plays perfectly into their answers.

Samsung recruited users who needed their product. That's working backwards from a problem.

SAMSUNG'S #S7MYPIC

Fun and altruism also works. Samsung is high up in the charts with consumers for lots of reasons. The product's everyday functionality is a huge part of their world. Smartphones have lots of reasons to connect—but what about a reach out with a sense of humor?

They proved that can be done with the release of their Galaxy S7. Their goal was to show consumers the crisp quality of the camera and its competitive qualities versus the iPhone. So they started reaching out to consumers who posted their photos on Instagram with popular hashtags.

If consumers knew they were posting a poorly lit photo or a grainy video, all they had to do was add the hashtag #S7mypic. Samsung reproduced the mundane photos with higher quality (of course), but also in a way that was slightly off, so when compared side-by-side they showed a sense of humor. For instance, a grainy photo of two women in a swimming pool is recreated by two men wearing wigs and bikini tops. A low-quality close up of a man drinking coffee is recreated with a man drinking from a pineapple. The bonus for participation? The consumer gets a chance to win the new phone.

The net of it is this: they recruited users who needed their product. That's working backwards from a problem.

CHIPOTLE HAIKU CONTEST

Writers, start your poems! Chipotle Burrito Love Haiku Contest has begun. Rules: chip.tl/HaikuRules -Joe

Chipotle set the stage for attitude and tonality by staging a one-day Haiku contest. They asked fans to write a haiku expressing their love for burritos, hashtag it to Twitter, or post it on the brand's Facebook page. The incredibly simple concept had simple prizing to match—just dinner for two at Chipotle.

This wasn't a big idea. There were only 20 prizes awarded. The connection platform made it easy for consumers to play along. The concept was fun and tapped into loyalists' love for the brand. And it got big social coverage.

JORDAN #RE2PECT

Jordan starts with a truth: they love sports and competition and so do their loyalists. So step back and admire how they connected the dots. In the anticipation of Derek Jeter's final season before retirement, the Jordan brand started a multi-platform #RE2PECT campaign to pay homage to one of baseball's legends.

What began as a :90 iconic spot that was released on Facebook, YouTube and Twitter, would soon become a phenomenon. Just as Michael Jordan tipped his cap, fans were called to do the same, joining a lineup of notable celebrities doing the same. Websites, celebrity followers—it all laddered up to the most shared video in the history of Facebook's native video player and reached 1,750,000 Instagram engagements.

Complete class. And the opportunity to participate alongside those celebrities you look up to. Who wouldn't want to tip their cap?

TOYOTA AT STAGECOACH

Sometimes it just takes joining the party. That's what Toyota did, leveraging a sponsorship with a lively tonality that filled social streams. Stagecoach is a country music-focused festival with a little less hype than Coachella, its sister event. But that made it perfect for Toyota to drive the social conversation by introducing a livestream on the perfect connection platform for this audience, Tumblr. They tied it all together with a thematic of "Music Moves You."

At the event, concertgoers could participate in shareworthy experiences through a skills course using a RAV4Rally car and a "Thrill Ride and Drive" event. Easy connections—not forced ones. And the band played on.

DR PEPPER #PICKYOURPEPPER UNIQUE PACKAGES

Dr Pepper is for individuals, people who cherish their own self-expression. And to make it happen, they used advanced printing technology to apply a unique text, patterns and logo to each package (at a mass scale!). That meant each store was filled with unique packages to choose from.

The digital campaign centered on the hashtag #Pickyourpepper and drove users to a site where they could explore the many package designs and create their own shareable animated GIF using a selection of patterns, logos and animations.

Either way, every 20oz is unique and everyone gets a chance to express themselves. This played well for trial, connectivity and ultimately endorsement through online sharing. And for the first time, they let go of their brand equity and made it about consumers. They could make up to 4,000 different designs, so everyone can truly Pick Their Pepper—certainly a brand goal. Not fancy. Just personalized.

FORD FIESTAGRAM

Ford deserves the credit for a very logical, but still original, concept that models co-creation.

Very simply, they wanted to communicate the technological features of the Ford Fiesta. And they identified influencers— in the territories of fashion, style and technology—as the ideal connection platform.

Certainly, a Fiesta wouldn't be the first thing to come to mind for these Instagram stars. And it certainly wouldn't be seen as genuine if those influencers started posting about points of difference of a Ford.

So Ford turned the attention back on their consumer. What do they want to see in their feeds? What do they want to share? They hosted a weekly photo contest on Instagram with a different, abstracted Fiesta feature as each week's theme (think #hidden or #music). They encouraged broad interpretation of the theme, celebrating photos of doorways and sunrises for entry.

There were weekly prizes, of course, with prizes that matched the territories they were trying to tap into, like iPads and digital cameras. The grand prize was naturally a Ford Fiesta. But they also featured the best entries in real-life galleries and digital out-of-home boards.

The campaign generated relevancy and a conversation around product benefits in a new way. Users submitted photos—awareness followed—and status shared.

All that to say that the Ford Fiesta has some new features. But remember, they didn't say it. They enabled influencers to create content that said it for them.

NORDSTROM STUDY BREAK

Activating a brand on Snapchat is an ongoing challenge, but the credibility that can be gained makes up for it. Nordstrom wanted to reach out to a younger audience—they need it to solidify their future (so they don't end up like irrelevant, aging giant Sears).

Snaps may be fleeting, but they asked consumers to screenshot the name of any of four schools whose names popped up on Nordstrom's story. The school whose name was snapped the most won an on-campus shoe party (hosted by supermodel Karli Kloss) and shoes to wear to interviews.

The connection platform was not only where these consumers were, but it was also fairly untapped by advertisers. But the original idea won permission. They tapped into school pride and competitive spirit by pitting the schools against each other and borrowed equity from Karli Kloss and $200,000 worth of shoe vouchers.

Drive intent. Drive relevancy. And all this while counting on consumers to be adept at snapping, screen-shotting and wanting to connect. Their Snapchat audience grew—and the shoes fit.

The importance of the original idea is indisputable. If you skip it and jump straight to the connection platform,

YOU'RE JUST PLAYING A TACTICS GAME.

But in today's digitally driven environment, if you stop at the original idea, you miss the opportunity to drive deeper brand connections with two-way participation.

PUT THE IDEAS INTO
PLAY

*Let's look at how you can not only generate that
great idea but also put it into use in the right
channel in a way that sparks participation.*

THOUGHT STARTER EXERCISE

Objective:
Earn the attention of your audience, and then return it to drive deeper brand connections.

Participation Game Strategy:
Focus on finding permission-worthy, original ideas and building on them to create the deep connections that result from two-way participation.

Thought Starters:
How can you give your audience the attention they crave in order to gain their participation? Think about:

- *Starting with Permission: what about your brand would give you the permission to communicate with your consumers? (Remember how Samsung provided a solution to a consumer challenge taking clear, sharp photos with their mobile devices.)*

- *Building on it with a Platform: in order to speak your audience's language, think about what language they speak. How do they communicate? (Think about how Wendy's leveraged a familiar symbol and let the audience choose which social channel to use.)*

- *Driving deeper connections with Participation: How can you celebrate and reward them for content they create? (Think about how Chipotle made poets out of their fans.)*

Notes:
....
....
....
....
....
....
....
....
....
....
....
....
....
....
....
....
....
....
....
....
....
....

Notes:

CHAPTER FIVE

MAKE ME LOOK GOOD, MAKE ME FEEL GOOD KEEP ME ENTERTAINED

After our first year of talking to consumers, we got introspective and wondered if we've been asking the wrong questions. Our research partner suggested we do some focus groups to understand, in consumers' own words, what is important to them.

We started with an empty white board and let them tell us. Later we went back and ranked the characteristics with larger groups.

MAKE ME LOOK GOOD:
BUILD THEIR BRAND TO WIN

We also started analyzing engagement by categories. We asked about what was holding their interest. Where did they spend their time? We saw that categories differed by engagement.

IN OTHER WORDS, THEY LIKE WHAT THEY LIKE.

We were particularly interested in why spirits and beer had lost their badge value to consumers. What we saw was that apparel and entertainment had the most engagement. But why?

ENGAGEMENT DIFFERS BY CATEGORY

Apparel and entertainment lead audience engagement across channels

BEER AND WINE

36%

Highest Engagement
FACEBOOK

SPIRITS

33%

Highest Engagement
IN PERSON
W.O.M.

CPG

50%

Highest Engagement
SEE AND TOUCH
WRITTEN REVIEWS

APPAREL

62%

Highest Engagement
SEE AND TOUCH

ENTERTAINMENT

62%

Highest Engagement
WRITTEN REVIEWS
W.O.M.

We learned two things from this. First was the importance of being high quality—inherent quality is a given. It's expected, essentially their baseline. And second,

IT'S ABOUT THEM.

Your brand has to improve their brand.

When we went back, we ranked these brand qualities with thousands of consumers.

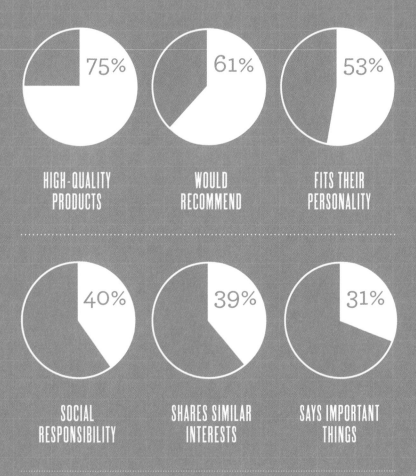

important brand characteristics

FOR MILLENNIALS

75%
HIGH-QUALITY
PRODUCTS

61%
WOULD
RECOMMEND

53%
FITS THEIR
PERSONALITY

40%
SOCIAL
RESPONSIBILITY

39%
SHARES SIMILAR
INTERESTS

31%
SAYS IMPORTANT
THINGS

MAKE ME FEEL GOOD
(ABOUT MYSELF AND THE WORLD)

What does it take for a brand to instill more than confidence in a consumer, but to actually give them that warm and fuzzy feeling inside? Hint: it's more than a charity program.

Today's consumers want brands that don't just throw money at causes. They want brands they can feel good about supporting as a whole. That means saying important things that your consumer agrees with—taking a stand when it comes to causes or values and sticking to them. It means being socially responsible. Doing the right thing as a brand.

The big ones that come to mind are brands like TOMS and Warby Parker, who have redefined their respective industries by giving a product to the needy for every product sold. If consumers feel like they're making a difference by engaging with your brand, then they feel good.

But it's also worth noting that we see brands like Seventh Generation showing up in our top brands surveys. They're not doing a lot of activation or putting a lot of media support behind their brand, but consumers see that they're a brand that can be trusted. They're taking a stand for a social cause (the environment) and being true to it. That's a strong way to win today.

TODAY'S CONSUMERS WANT BRANDS THAT DON'T JUST THROW MONEY AT CAUSES. THEY WANT BRANDS THEY CAN FEEL GOOD ABOUT SUPPORTING AS A WHOLE.

ENTERTAIN ME
(OR GET OUT OF MY LIFE)

I attended a panel recently and one of the students from the University of San Francisco stood up and said,

"IF YOU DON'T ENTERTAIN ME BY NINE IN THE MORNING, I WANT NOTHING TO DO WITH YOUR BRAND."

A report shared by Adobe recently said that 64% of consumers surveyed across six countries share content online. Among those who share external content, such as articles and photos, the top motivation is to make people laugh (37%), indicating an affinity for humorous and entertaining content from brands.

IN MY SOCIAL FEED I WANT TO SEE THINGS THAT

ARE FUN
AND INTERESTING

VS

6/1

HELP ME LEARN MORE ABOUT
PRODUCTS/SERVICES
COMPANIES

ENTERTAIN ME (OR GET OUT OF MY LIFE)

///

So it was no surprise that consumers told us they prefer fun and entertaining content six to one over news and information.

....

The fine line is to keep building your brand while meeting the criteria to be a part of their brand. If you're not an entertainment or retail brand, borrowing from entertainment is a major consideration. But keeping it genuine will get harder and harder to do.

When a brand says, "Fine, I'll just put my name on entertaining content from a publisher," are they really building anything? Do they really gain any inroads with consumers? Isn't that just another form of advertising? So keeping your personality while building theirs is the opportunity and the challenge.

*So keeping
your personality*

WHILE
BUILDING
THEIRS

*is the opportunity
and the challenge.*

as you read this,

CONSUMERS WILL POST
THREE TIMES

*as many videos
as last year.*

PERSONAL CONTENT
ALWAYS BEATS BRAND CONTENT

How is it that someone like Jen Selter, affectionately known as Butt Girl on Instagram, has 10M followers and gets over 200,000 likes every time she takes a picture of herself? Compare that to a mega-brand like Grey Goose, with a $30 million brand spend who gets maybe 1,000 likes on a cocktail shot on Instagram.

Personal video content continues to be the badge. As you read this, consumers will post three times as many videos as last year.

So what's next? Where's the rub? How do brands thread the needle and make it happen?

It's as if you should treat the key consumer takeaway for all marketing like a fortune cookie. But instead of adding the words "in bed," you should tack on, "makes me look good, makes me feel good, entertains me."

These three buckets are a thought starter for every brainstorm for us. How can we answer what consumers want within this framework?

let's look at some case studies so we can work backwards ·············▸

DISNEY'S MAD HATTER INTERACTIVE BILLBOARD

Disney came up with an idea to break through the imaginary wall with their promotion of *Through the Looking Glass,* the *Alice in Wonderland* sequel. They staged it at Disneyland and turned what appeared to be an out-of-home sign into an entertaining interactive experience that consumers would feel compelled to share.

Johnny Depp was in-character as the Mad Hatter in a studio, but with the use of a secret camera and live stream technology, he was able to interact with theme park viewers, surprising and delighting park guests. Of course, the stunt became an entertaining video, and it received over 16 million views on Facebook and YouTube and was shared more than 200,000 times.

Why did it work? They maintained their brand to a tee, but they used interactivity to make it about the consumer (their message was secondary), all while packaging it in an entertaining and shareable format.

WALMART GREENLIGHT A VET

Leveraging feel-good opportunities means doing it with a genuine approach that makes the exchange of information feel seamless. Walmart showed great class and intuition by recognizing an important issue: veterans who are making the transition out of uniform need everyone's support.

The "Greenlight A Vet" campaign captured hearts with a simple concept. In order to illuminate that vets are not always visible, Walmart encouraged consumers to change a lightbulb to a special green one, providing an original way for communities and households to join a movement and show their support.

The campaign released five videos exploring the lives of different veterans, so consumers connected their action with real feelings, and viewers were encouraged to share those moving stories. They also encouraged consumers to post photos of their greenlight with #greenlightvet—and the opportunity for two-way participation was perfectly executed.

Additionally, Walmart did their part and made a pledge to the Veterans Welcome Home Commitment, promising to hire 250,000 veterans by the year 2020. With the campaign fully grounded, and of course green light bulbs available at Walmart, they turned to TV and Times Square to let consumers feel the momentum leading up to Veteran's Day.

AMAZON'S BIGGEST PRIME BOX EVER

Amazon wins consumer adoration on a number of fronts. They can do ecommerce and get a transaction conversation going. They can reward frequent purchasers. They can promote

one of the key benefits of their Prime product, video content, and entertain members with movies and TV shows.

Tying in with Jet Blue then, was a solid strategic move—their customers are colorful, adventurous and value their status. Amazon brought it all together connecting to Jet Blue's inflight Fly-Fi service. Streaming all of Amazon's content in their air is a feat into itself—and they pulled that off. Prime members got that. Others were encouraged to join Prime or at least sample the product for a small fee while in the air.

To bring it to life on the ground, they set up the "Biggest Prime Box Ever" in JFK's Terminal 5. The pop up activation consisted of a large glass box with benches and headphones so that passersby could experience Fly-Fi's offerings. In addition, a kids area allowed children to watch Amazon's original childrens series.

Ultimately, the result was a massive experiential sampling concept that borrowed cache from Jet Blue and delivered an intuitive, entertaining impression—when weary and bored travelers needed entertainment the most.

APPLE'S SHOT ON AN iPHONE

Apple plays in every zone—it's entertainment, connectivity, everyday functionality and certainly the on-going evolution of new technology. Their brand has badge value (make me look good), their device connects to friends and loved ones (make me feel good) and it enables all kinds of games, videos and social engagement (entertain me).

They built the brand with groundbreaking, buzzworthy technology. But when the iPhone 6 was coming into the market, the camera turned back to consumers.

Photography belongs to everyone, and certainly the idea that your phone camera is a great one can be debated. But Apple started a movement by featuring user generated content with its "Shot on iPhone" campaign. It literally turned the world into a gallery using the photos and videos of 162 different users. The content was strategically placed across all mediums—creating a 360° message.

It's the epitome of a 'make me look good' activation. The focus was on the consumer—and why not, they believe already that they're worthy of all that attention. Their photos and videos are the most important thing to them. Look what others are doing and start showing off. They're currently in the seven billion impression range and have a 95% positive mention metric. It's clear that consumers need their phone to build status. Apple just wants it to be an iPhone.

MICHAEL KORS WATCH HUNGER STOP

Consider taking a category's name and turning it into a verb that pretty much makes the conversation about your brand.

Michael Kors did that with "Watch Hunger Stop", a smart 'make me feel good' concept. He was named Global Ambassador Against World Hunger for the United Nations World Food Program, certainly setting an example of compassion and character.

The program was three short words and one huge idea. Trading up to a limited edition Michael Kors watch came with more than a promise of quality. Engraved into each watch was the phrase "1 watch equals 100 meals." Each purchase meant that 100 meals would be delivered to children living in places like Cambodia, Mozambique, Nicagarua and Uganda.

But you didn't have to buy a watch to participate. Originally, the website offered consumers the ability to upload a selfie, finish the phrase "Today I want to…" and generate a shareable image of themselves with a virtual, branded t-shirt with their custom message. Take part and Michael Kors would donate 50 meals on your behalf.

But after a few years of successful execution, they've upgraded the engagement. Download the app and tap daily for a 50-cent donation. Or go to their brick-and-mortar store—on a designated day, you can use a Snapchat geo-filter to spark a 25-meal donation. And some stores will distribute free t-shirts. Hashtag a selfie while wearing your shirt and Michael Kors will donate 25 meals.

They're saying something important and supporting a cause that matters, and they're doing it in a way that links directly back to their brand (and drives traffic in store), all the while letting consumers impact the cause. After all, the brand may be making the donation but it's the consumers who are instigating them, right?

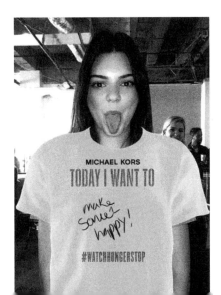

CHEVROLET #BESTDAYEVER

The axiom of surprise and delight was certainly the inspiration for Chevrolet, as they looked to launch and reveal their new model releases.

Through partnerships with charities, celebrities and schools, they orchestrated a single day of pure excitement and social sharing called #Bestdayever that delivered on "make me feel good" and "entertain me."

The entire day was themed "Acts of Awesomeness" and featured celebrities surprising consumers with unexpected moments of joy. Alec Baldwin dressed as Abraham Lincoln and showed up at a history class. Kelly Clarkson gave a surprise concert to pregnant moms. Danica Patrick gave out gas cards.

The entire event took eight hours and was featured on the brand's YouTube channel, generating more than three million views and ultimately more than 1.5 billion impressions.

The playfulness and unexpected rewards obviously were the most opportunistic way to get consumers to share their brand with Chevy's. Who wouldn't want to be the first to tell their friends what they just saw? And if they are, Chevy gets to tap into the "make me look good" axiom, too.

Ultimately, the breadcrumb is there for consumers to follow.

CHAPTER

5

PUT THE IDEAS INTO
PLAY

*The moral of this chapter's story is simple: make them
look good, make them feel good or entertain them. And you'll
see even better response if you can deliver on more than one
of those important tenets. Just be sure you're building
your brand while building theirs.*

THOUGHT STARTER EXERCISE

Objective:
Provide the value your consumers want.

Participation Game Strategy:
How can you turn your messaging on its head, making it first about your audience while remaining genuinely from you.

Thought Starters:
How can your brand make your audience look good? Think about:

- *How can your brand fit into what the audience is already doing to build their individual brands?*

How can your brand make your audience feel good? Think about:

- *What important things can your brand say?*

- *What social causes are important to your audience? How can they genuinely relate to your brand?*

How can your brand entertain your audience? Think about:

- *What type(s) of entertainment does your audience prefer (humor, inspirational or moving, thought-provoking, etc.) What tonality fits within the voice of your brand?*

- *What entertainment properties are appealing to your audience? How can you leverage them without losing your own brand identity?*

Notes:

....
....
....
....
....
....
....
....
....
....
....
....
....
....
....
....
....
....
....
....
....
....
....

Notes:

CHAPTER SIX

PLAY FOR
KEEPS

*There's a new filter that connects consumers to brands.
It's called Play.*

*Here's why: Consumers feel they are constantly
in a game—a challenge by the very nature of social
media. Who had the most likes? Who is "winning"
Instagram today?*

But how does a brand play with consumers without triggering the advertising alarm and losing their attention? There are three effective ways that we brainstorm: challenge your consumers, have fun with them or live in their zone.

There's a new filter that connects consumers to brands.

IT'S CALLED PLAY.

Challenge your consumers.
They hate to lose. So what happens when you mesh it up—mix up branding, gaming and lifestyle, and you'll be in the right space.

Have fun with them.
Be the cruise director. Constantly start each day with that "entertain me by nine a.m." mentality.

Live in their zone.
Continue to surface the things that your consumers care about and drive some passion with it.

play with

CONSUMERS

CHALLENGE
THEM

HAVE FUN
WITH THEM

LIVE IN
THEIR ZONE

HARNESSING THE POWER OF
INFLUENCERS

HP knows how to have fun with their consumers, entertaining them while living in their zone. They partner with influencers, people trusted by the communities they are trying to reach. But, to reiterate the point Vikrant Batra made in an earlier chapter, they are careful not to force it. They allow the influencers to keep it authentic.

For example, in 2014 HP was launching their bendy laptop (a laptop with a keyboard that could flip around completely to become a sort of tablet stand). Twitter's micro-video platform, Vine, was gaining traction, so HP partnered with five of its top stars. And they kept the brief simple: do what you know how to do, and show that the laptop bends. Robby Ayala's video showed him watching a young woman bending her HP laptop in half. In response, he tries to do the same with his Acer laptop and ends up breaking it. The short, 6-second clip became the most watched branded piece of content in Vine's history, with upward of 10-million loops.

It's just like with HP's surf documentary that we discussed in Chapter One. Include your brand, but make it about them. HP actually followed up the seven-minute surf doc with more surf-related content—living in their zone isn't a one and done kind of thing. They found a surf shop that creates custom boards, and they filmed a three-minute video showing how the surfboard designers involve their customers in the design process—of course using HP's Sprout computer.

The story wasn't about the technology though. It was about designing surfboards.

IT'S NOT ABOUT YOU— IT'S ABOUT THEM.

IT'S ABOUT THE INFLUENCERS,

the consumers and what they care about first and foremost.

We did something similar with Sapporo beer. We partnered with Motomatic, an authentic shop that makes custom mopeds. We let them design 30 original mopeds that we gave away to consumers. Along the way, we captured great video content of these craftsmen talking about their passions. Of course, there was a parallel between the passion and craftsmanship that goes into making Sapporo, but that's all implied subtext. It's about the influencers, the consumers and what they care about first and foremost.

TAPPING INTO
GAMING CULTURE

Gaming will always be popular, and there's always new ways to challenge. Look at the way Pokémon Go literally blew up overnight and gained 100 million users in a single week. If that's not a sign that consumers are craving a challenge, I don't know what is.

Take a note from the gamers behind the Minecraft brand. They've spurred an incredible online community. They are successfully teaching consumers how to upload videos of their creative experience, literally how to record yourself playing the game and upload it to YouTube. The end result is more videos being uploaded for their game than any game in history, and a wide user base that teach each other how to get more immersed in the brand every day. It's a co-creation, entertainment zone that will continue to expand, not only with platforms, but with consumer imagination.

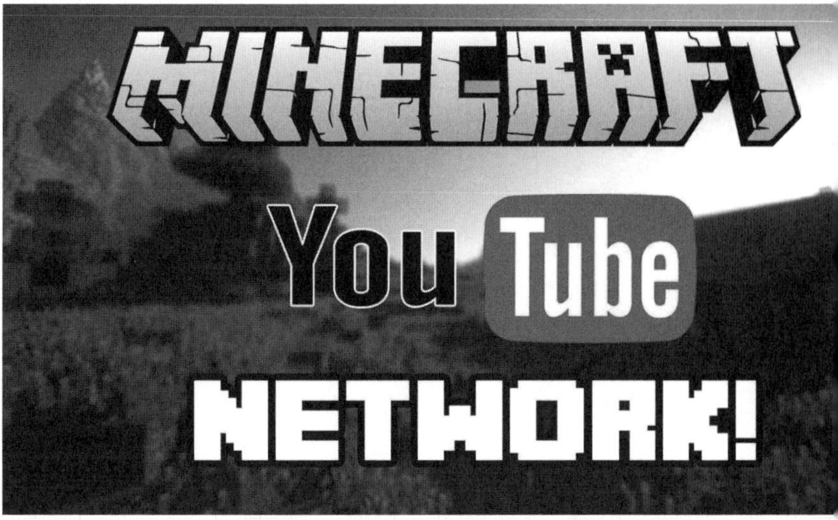
MINECRAFT
YouTube
NETWORK!

TIGHTEN THE
CONNECTION

Engaging in a game tightens the connection. You can provide value that they need in order to achieve their goal.

They have dropped the advertiser filter and let you in. Think about the ESPN app for fantasy football. Push notifications are necessary. Consumers actually *want* to get pinged all day. The brand literally becomes their partner.

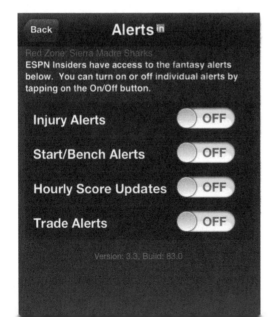

you are a

MARKETER MARKETING TO A MARKETER.

*consumers use your brand
to brand their brand.*

WHAT'S YOUR VALUE?

take a look at a few brands that are getting it right ········▶

FORD'S ESCAPE THE ROOM

Ford used gaming and technology to re-invent the test drive.

Escape the Room is an immersive, interactive experience that requires players to use technology and gaming skills— a group of consumers go into a game room and willingly get locked in. They can get out by solving puzzles using clues that are built into the room's décor and contents. It's growing and in multiple cities. It also shares part of its name with one of Ford's most popular models. So it was a perfect opportunity for Ford Escape to bridge the gap between what's in it for them and what's in it for consumers.

They worked with "visionary puzzle master" Victor Blake to create the largest single escape experience in a 35,000 square foot venue in New York City. They then offered 1,000 consumers the chance to play—and they had them, with a sellout within 24 hours.

The car's technology features, such as the Sony audio system and iHeart Radio streaming music, were integrated in the game to make sure they had all of the content and components working hard for them. They tied in with New York State's "I Love New York" campaign so consumers would truly learn about parts of their state they didn't know about. And they learned to love a car they hadn't even driven yet.

To get from room to room, participants had to use the SUV's capabilities—overcoming obstacles and learning about the vehicle's unique assets, like remote start and lock or voice-to- text capabilities. After the experience, the footage of their personal game was turned into a branded video and sent to each participant to share on social media.

Compare this to a traditional awareness funnel in the automotive industry. Consumer sees a commercial and is encouraged to take a test drive. Instead they see this dynamic experience in their friend's feed. The friend has done something to brag about and Ford is endorsed.

BMW'S EYES ON GIGI

Gaming gets attention—and BMW leveraged its style and creativity with a new spin on the classic "shell game."

The basic concept: watch a super model get into a new BMW M2 in its inaugural year. Then put four identical cars on a track and keep your eyes on her. When the high-speed shell game ends, identify the car she's in.

The model was Gigi Hadid—who already brought 15 million Instagram followers with her and almost two million Twitter fans. Couple that with BMW's existing fans and add in the director of *World War Z* and *Quantum Solace*. Oh, and you could play along with a standard video, or you could try it in 360°, swiveling your smartphone around to keep track of the fast-paced cars.

Everything laddered up to the gaming site EyesonGigi.com, where users could see if they've guessed the correct car and, of course, learn about the new M2 coupe.

NIKE FUEL VENDING MACHINE

Nike has always had an edge with technology and style, maintaining their popularity by never being dull. They innovated early on with the FuelBand, then brought it to a social stunt that set the bar.

The concept of a vending machine that consumers interact with makes sense—but they did it with FuelBand points. Unlike BMW, consumers needed the product to participate. They needed to use it.

Nike secretly put a branded vending machine in New York City. The machine only dispensed Nike gear, and players only got it by paying with daily FuelBand points.

The machine was moved daily to surprise locations and consumers could follow its location on Twitter. Nike expects its consumers to work hard at fitness, so the rewards were for those who do the work. Their values came to life on a gaming platform that set the tone for other brands.

JCPENNEY PLAY TO GIVE

Who doesn't want to go to an Oscar party? JCPenney connected the dots between the fashion they sell, celebrities and a reason for connecting with a watch-and-win game called "Play to Give."

Recognizing that consumers were going to be having a second screen experience with or without them, they put together a game board that consumers could sign up to play. Check that: they made the connection and then sent an email and made social contact.

They then allowed consumers to play along with the Oscars, selecting moments of the night to correspond to the game. As consumers earned points, all of their efforts were rewarded with donations to one of three charities. Second check: share the values for a good cause.

All of this laddered back to the clothing and style that are available at JCPenney. They challenged their consumers, they're having fun, they're in the zone and everyone wins.

SONY PLAYSTATION MOBILE GAME

Sony Playstation is always ready to play with consumers. But their world is just as competitive—having to define their relevance and allow consumers to give them the street cred they need to compete.

To build that cred, they created a free mobile game to hype the release of the brand's Uncharted 4: A Thief's End PlayStation Game. The free app, Uncharted 4: Fortune Hunter, allowed consumers to play the mobile game before the full game's release—and to earn points and build buzz along the way.

The mobile app was a puzzle game consisting of six different adventures. Consumers could earn "keys" from each puzzle, which in turn unlocked points to be used with the forthcoming console game.

Bread crumbs. A free connection on mobile. And a ready audience for a roll out.

HONDA STAGE

Sometimes it's not one promotion or theme—but an on-going effort to build an audience. Honda has grown its user base with a gaming platform that shows they understand the values and attention span of their audience.

They started showing up on the radar with interactive videos for the Civic, allowing consumers to click between day and night videos on YouTube to watch a story evolve. The idea was to simulate the experience and used the technology of that time to establish itself as an intuitive connector.

All this connected back to their YouTube channel—and additional promotion through music venues. But the promotions kept coming. Music venues, behind the scenes videos and exclusive content all continue to build relevance and consistency which builds brand affinity.

To top it off, they partnered with gaming-themed video portal Machinima to integrate the Honda Fit into its 13-episode Street Fighter Assassin's Fist web series. The smart thing here is that it was more than a simple product placement. Fans of the original game knew (and loved) that during bonus rounds players got to let loose on a generic car, so it was a clever and in-the-know reference to include their product in the webisodes.

NETFLIX HOUSE OF CARDS
#FU2016

Consumers told us in our surveys they are watching TV for one to four hours a day. Only a third of it is live and the rest is on recorded shows.

With this type of exposure, the characters take on a life of their own. So when Netflix wanted to promote the fourth season of *House of Cards*, what better way to do it in an election year, but to trot Frank Underwood out for a victory lap?

Netflix brought it all to real life with a real election headquarters in Greenville, South Carolina. The location—right across the street from the Republican primary debate—also happened to be the home state of the fictional character.

The kicker: the campaign theme captured the way consumers feel about reality. The character running for president was Frank Underwood, so it became #FU2016. Consumers could take photos in an oval office replica or visit the campaign website.

The experience continued seamlessly online with digital tools to add fuel to the fire of the election chaos. The multi-faceted campaign included videos, shareable social content and, of course, merchandise to show support. Having fun with consumers and bringing them a reason to share their fervor for Frank paid off.

VERIZON'S MINECRAFT INTEGRATION

Verizon and Minecraft crossed the streams. They worked together to put real, working smartphone capability into the Minecraft gaming platform.

The product placement enhanced gameplay in a way gamers hadn't seen before. They could actually make video calls from within the game, with the recipient shown on the Verizon phone inside the game in Minecraft's signature, blocky style. And of course, the recipient would see the caller on their screen (outside of the game) in Minecraft style too. In this new capability, gamers can do everything from send selfies and surf the web to order a pizza—all without leaving the game.

The result amazed gamers, which is hard to do. They're the most sophisticated of them all. The third party endorsement makes them a hero to the gaming community with comments like "insane." You can't force that kind of feedback from the most clever TV commercials. You only get it by pushing the envelope.

All of this laddered up to support Verizon's "Better Matters" campaign and was live-streamed and showcased by various Minecraft super users, who were able to demonstrate the features. That built buzz, provided value to the audience and showed a brand that plays with its consumers in their zone.

How should brands incorporate gaming into their platforms? How can it feel organic and not forced? Consider getting the strategy articulated first—work backwards from the need to connect on a relevant platform. The ideas need to come first.

THE FEELING HAS TO BE REAL.

But gaming solves a lot of credibility problems in one fell swoop—as long as brands don't try too hard.

CHAPTER

6

PUT THE IDEAS INTO PLAY

Challenge consumers—giving them a chance to play softens the messaging. Connecting with on-going information and content erases advertiser status and turns it into friendship. Give it a try.

THOUGHT STARTER EXERCISE

Objective:
Be an active part of your audience's lifestyle.

Participation Game Strategy:
The days of expecting consumers to come to you are over—brands need to take part in their lifestyles. So let's look at the ways your brand can challenge consumers and have fun with them on their level.

Thought Starters:
How can your brand connect to your consumers' passions, hobbies and, even, time wasters? Think about:

- *How do your consumers' spend their free time? Can your brand enhance it? Or how can your brand show you care about it?*

- *How can you play with your consumers? How can you challenge them and incite their competitive spirit?*

Notes:
....
....
....
....
....
....
....
....
....
....
....
....
....
....
....
....
....
....
....
....
....
....
....
....
....
....
....

Notes:

CHAPTER SEVEN

THERE'S NO SUCH THING AS
BRANDED CONTENT

In the previous chapter, we saw how fun and games get consumers involved and rope them into the brand. All content has to be something the consumer cares about, or at least be served up in a way that they will care about. Consumers didn't care what the features were on the Ford Escape until it helped them get out of The Escape Room.

What's next? How do you engage on a level that brings admiration for your brand? What inspires it?

A lot of brands and a lot of agencies talk about content. They add the word brand to it.

SO NOW WE HAVE A THING CALLED BRANDED CONTENT.

What is that supposed to be?

This is a backward proposition. It's not something that consumers want. It's something that brands want: to somehow share their story in a relevant way.

Real admiration needs to be established—and that takes planning and grounding that's based on honesty.

When we asked consumers what characteristics a brand has to have for them to adopt, they all said, "fits my personality."

The challenge for brands is that this cannot be a check box. The concept and connection need to forge a deep connection. It can be a tough way for marketers to think. Even though the brand manager may be judged on sales, consumers are judging on relevancy.

Here's the thing: it doesn't always have to be serious. Sometimes it can show you have a sense of humor. Just as long as you show who you are, you're doing the job.

When we asked consumers what characteristics a brand has to have for them to adopt, they all said,

"FITS MY PERSONALITY."

let's take a look at a few ways to get that done ·······························▶

OLD NAVY NEVER BASIC

With a brand that has limited new news, Gap's Old Navy division needed to reinvent its relevancy and make itself useful to consumers. Think about the brief: sell more basic t-shirts. That's it.

They call the brand basic. How does that serve consumers?

They went at it two ways. One was an interactive campaign in which consumers could participate in a "wearable art" project from artist Paulina Sotto. For a launch event, she created basic stencils of simple geometric patterns that could be applied to any of four new shirts that consumers could purchase. Of course they were encouraged to post to the #neverbasic Instagram feed.

To drive it home, they enlisted former Saturday Night Live cast members to articulate off-the-wall messages about originality in their "basic" t-shirts. With a quirky, humorous tone and a strong digital presence, they ensured shareable content.

To what end? Just creating a conversation where there is none. This campaign got mixed reviews—but the fact that people were talking at all about basic t-shirts, did the job.

Was it just traditional advertising with a funny theme? Getting it to shareable content by pushing the envelope and then allowing for consumers to join in moves it toward the fourth quadrant. This was a tough brief. The brand is basic. The product is basic. But the concept was intuitive. It's a relief to know you don't have to spend a lot to be interesting.

NIKE KY-RISPIE KREME

In the world of why not, Nike connected its endorsement from Cleveland Cavelier's point guard Kyrie Irving to a random thought. Why not invent the "Ky-Rispie Kreme" and introduce the new shoes with a twist?

They executed the complete package—endearing them to consumers with videos that featured Kyrie serving up donuts. The shoes were delivered in a special donut box. In addition, the tour featured a Krispy Kreme-inspired truck that gave away free donuts to consumers.

What's the DNA? Take a simple idea and make it real. Don't take yourself too seriously. Reward consumers for playing along. Would you have predicted Nike would partner with a donut brand? Doing so was unexpected but made it attention grabbing and more entertaining.

Step back the next time you have a brief and ask yourself, what can you do that re-invents the reason for being?

They could have easily taken themselves at face value. But that's not how consumers take Kyrie or their love of playing and watching sports.

CHICK-FIL-A COW APPRECIATION DAY

In the context of brand campaigns, the "Eat Mor Chikin" concept had incredible longevity. Allowing consumers to participate in the fun can only prolong it, and the chain did just that by creating an annual "Cow Appreciation Day."

So we are far from reality but it's their reality and consumers were happy to join in. They could dress like cows and receive a free meal when they visited the store. All of this flowed right into social and created the suspension of disbelief. Yes, they do appreciate cows.

NORTH FACE
#NEVERSTOPEXPLORING

North Face is not trying to be funny—they're trying to be a part of their loyalists' lifestyles. They created a global campaign and enlisted athletes, including mountaineers and snowboarders, to share stories of their personal exploration.

A very simple concept site, neverstopexploring.com, gives consumers an opportunity to participate with their brand by sharing stories and photos to win a $100 prize. The website says very clearly, A PURCHASE IS REQUIRED.

They are selling products on the site but they're still sincerely letting consumers be a part of the brand. They're getting out of the way and letting the content focus on the consumers.

They're backing it up with a speaker series, which consists of athletes traveling to cities across the US to inspire consumers who are looking for inspiration.

Their products don't fool around. They're the real deal. The brand's participatory programming delivers the same tonality.

TACO BELL TACO EMOJI

It started as a lark. Someone at Taco Bell said there needs to be a taco emoji on the standard Apple keyboard. They started a petition with change.org. They seriously commiserated with consumers who were in the mood for tacos and needed to be able to simply share their emotions.

The effort took over a year and the reward was huge. With the new emoji, they released a slew of new content—600 images that consumers could include in their shares and get instant tweet-backs to win prizes.

The tweet-backs were equally as creative and surprising. Tacos are not serious. But getting consumers to participate was serious business.

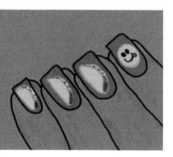 

The more messages and opportunities they get, the harder it is for brands to break through the stream and be a part of the mix. Once that happens, the consumer's mission takes a life of its own.

AND THAT'S THE KEY TO SHAREABLE CONTENT.

PUT THE IDEAS INTO
PLAY

*The judge of "fits my personality" is the consumer.
As you ideate on content, use the consumer as your first
and most important filter.*

THOUGHT STARTER EXERCISE

Objective:

Use content to show (rather than tell) your brand story and values in an entertaining or engaging way.

Participation Game Strategy:

In Chapter 7, we dove more deeply into the idea of content—simply adding a brand placement or sponsorship doesn't make branded content work. Building on the "entertain me" idea from Chapter 5, let's look at how can your brand produce content that is both what your audience wants to see and builds your brand.

Thought Starters:

How can your brand create relevancy, proving it fits your audience's personality? Think about:

- *Can you leverage equity from other things your consumer cares about?*

- *What are the things your brand genuinely has permission to talk about? What are intrinsic and extrinsic truths of your brand? What equities does your brand have?*

- *What are consumers already doing with your brand? Can you build off that in a new or interesting way?*

Notes:

....
....
....
....
....
....
....
....
....
....
....
....
....
....
....
....
....
....
....
....
....
....
....

Notes:

....
....
....
....
....
....
....
....
....
....
....
....
....
....
....
....
....
....
....
....
....
....
....
....
....
....
....
....
....
....

CHAPTER EIGHT

SHARING IS CARING

We talked about Kevin Roberts and Lovemarks as we worked our way out of the '90s. Where did we end up? The consumer wants to have fun, participate, get retweeted, enjoy brands. The only type of connectivity that sticks is through their lens.

Roberts said, "Make them laugh. Make them cry. Make them think."

Now we add one caveat: Make them share.

There is literally no purpose for social to serve advertisers.

ITS INTENT IS TO SERVE FRIENDS AND FRIENDS OF FRIENDS.

A brand does not get a free pass from the platforms. The unpaid reach for a brand post is incredibly narrow. But sharing does get a pass. When connection platforms like Facebook and its subsidiary Instagram, as well as Twitter, say they reward relevancy when it comes to brand content, they're talking about what's getting shared. Their algorithms are tuned to original content—the kind that comes from consumers. So when your content comes from consumers, you win.

Consumers will be more creative than ever going forward. Technology is making it easier and easier for them to show their creative chops, experiment and surprise and delight their friends. What does that tell us? The puck is moving to video. Consumers will be there—so brand communication will need to make that change. For brands, that means co-creating with your consumers.

When content generated by (or with) a brand is shared by a consumer, the connection platforms treat it as original content. It gets the same reach as the photos consumers share of their kids—but it's a brand's voice.

So once you've achieved shareable content, the social platforms treat it as original. You've crossed the line to friendship.

We learned that most consumers want to hear from their favorite brand only 10% of the time. But we also learned that if they like the content, 30% said they would share it. Many times it's these breakthrough missions that connect most deeply with consumers and push brand loyalty to new levels.

SHARED CONTENT WILL GET TO ALMOST 100% OF YOUR TARGET'S TARGET.

Social Bakers provided these stats ························▶

for brands
SHARING IS CARING

facebook PAID SOCIAL FEED POSTING

COMMENTS

72%
Change of Reach

SHARE

99.8%
Change of Reach

facebook ORGANIC SOCIAL FEED POSTING

COMMENTS

28%
Change of Reach

SHARE

94%
Change of Reach

Source: Social Bakers | A study by MOOSYLVANIA ©2016 All Rights Reserved.

WHEN YOUR
CONTENT COMES
FROM CONSUMERS,
YOU WIN.

That means your content is getting attention, and it's the kind that matters: word of mouth. There is simply no comparison to traditional message delivery. The argument for more shareable content is pretty simple:

SHOW US THAT KIND OF EFFECTIVENESS ANYWHERE ELSE.

It's the endorsement that suddenly
turns the equation on its side.

It's the holy grail:
SHARING IS CARING.

the share effect

EXPONENTIAL REACH

....

IMPLIED
ENDORSEMENT

THE GAP'S CLOSE THE PAY GAP

Brands who take on long-term appeals to the public can find their voice and build relationships. There was a time when this was called "Cause Marketing."

That would be a little too blatant for today's consumer. What is working is when an authentic truth comes across with honesty and concern.

The Gap took this on with a site and a program called #closethepaygap, which identifies the enduring battle for equal pay for women.

They've created a microsite at equality.gapinc.com with educational content told in a compelling way and an online pay calculator. Users enter their age and it instantly computes the lifetime loss of pay, complete with a Facebook and Twitter button for instant sharing. They complete the story with tips on how to advocate for a pay raise.

Their ads show women missing 40% of their outfits—with bold statements that invoke participation. They're not creating an issue. It's one that exists. They're giving consumers a way to talk about it and change their own personal situation.

They aren't selling clothing. They're selling commitment.

VANS LIVING OFF THE WALL

Vans is a classic example of a company that uses its ad budget to connect with consumers. They're selling a lifestyle—and it's reflected in their brand motto, "Off The Wall."

It's on their website. It's their pledge. Staying on the theme, they created #livingoffthewall—the latest version of their long-running documentary series. They describe it as "...a state of mind. Thinking differently. Embracing creative self-expression."

The mission is to tell the story to their fans through video of their fans, to honor the spirit of originality. They invite everyone to join and share their own stories. Their blog-style site, livingoffthewall.com brings it home.

The organic nature of each video couldn't be bought. But it can definitely be shared.

GOOGLE SHARES THE PRIDE

When a company uses its assets for good, it creates an impression. Google assumed responsibility for the world to be able to attend Pride parades, regardless of their geographic and political situation.

They documented Pride parades using 360° technologies to create a VR montage for those unable to celebrate the LGBTQ community in person. Google recognized that in more than 70 countries, it is illegal to be gay, and in seeing this, wanted to send a strong message of equality.

The brand worked with various LGBTQ Googlers in 25 different countries to march and document local Pride parades over the course of several weeks. The footage was then made available on the YouTube360 and Google Cardboard platforms. They simply used their reach to become a mouthpiece for their consumers.

Forward thinking. Admirable. Shareable.

H&M CLOSE THE LOOP

Easily, H&M could have just done what they always do. Offer style at a price that excites consumers. But they went further and invested in a campaign to promote the importance of recycling clothing.

In their "Close the Loop" campaign, the only rule in fashion is to recycle your clothes. The campaign's film, which includes a diverse group of models (including plus-sized, transgender and amputee models), was shot in various locations around the world to promote global inclusivity.

The purpose: bring us your old clothes. We'll recycle them and reward you with a discount on your next purchase. H&M informed its audience that recycling just a t-shirt saves 2,100 liters of water. With Iggy Pop as the spokesperson, the video received over 10 million views.

Over 260 billion pounds of clothing were collected, but the efforts clearly outweighed the return on just sales—it was the return on goodwill they achieved.

CHASE MORNING BELL FOR SMALL BUSINESS

Chase Bank recognizes that small businesses are the lifeblood of the economy and promoted it with an on-going program called The Morning Bell for Small Business.

Entrepreneurs across the US were encouraged to submit videos, and Chase shared a new one every day. The concept is simple—since big businesses get to ring a bell every morning at the stock exchange, why not let small businesses do the same?

They are only asking for 20 seconds but will share quality submissions. So what happens when a small business gets mentioned? Of course, they share it.

At the bottom of the site, the natural appeal: "We're here to help you manage your money today and tomorrow." After this effort, we believe it.

CONVERSE MADE BY YOU

Made by You, a campaign from Converse to celebrate the Chuck Taylor All-Star's 100th birthday, highlights the people who made Chucks what they are today by asking them to customize pairs into artwork.

In New York, London and Shanghai, the brand set up art installations and murals showcasing the work of creatives. The galleries included everyone, from the famous like Warhol, to your neighbors. The customized sneakers appeared in video ads, and Converse asked fans to show off their own creations using the hashtag #ChuckTaylors.

Ultimately, what they got back was the human factor—the personalized feeling—whether it was just a classic well-worn pair or decorated art.

Converse knew equity belongs to the well-worn users—and they're happy to share it.

CHAPTER

9

PUT THE IDEAS INTO
PLAY

*Promoting through social and community-based intentions
takes honesty and integrity. It's not easy to get it to match up to
the bottom line. But in order to impact your bottom line, you've got
to get your audience's attention. And the best way to do that
is to get them to share—and create—on your behalf.*

THOUGHT STARTER EXERCISE

Objective:

Engage your consumers in
co-creation to get them sharing
on behalf of your brand.

Participation Game Strategy:

In Chapter 8, we looked at the power
of consumer sharing in today's digital
environment and the filter through
which consumers decide whether or
not to share—will their own audience
want to see it? Let's focus on creating
mechanisms that allow consumers
to share something valuable to them
about your brand.

Thought Starters:

What sort of share can your brand spark
that your audience's network of family
and friends will want to see in their
feeds? Think about:

- *What does it look like when your brand's message combines with your audience's personal message?*

- *How can you give consumers a mechanism to share their voice?*

- *What important causes does your consumer care about? In what genuine ways can you raise up (but not hijack) those messages?*

Notes:

....
....
....
....
....
....
....
....
....
....
....
....
....
....
....
....
....
....
....
....
....
....

Notes:

....
....
....
....
....
....
....
....
....
....
....
....
....
....
....
....
....
....
....
....
....
....
....
....
....
....
....
....
....
....

CHAPTER NINE

IT'S NOT YOUR TARGET MARKET

IT'S YOUR TARGET'S MARKET

As we saw earlier, it's more crowded then ever before. But now you understand how important the genuine, two-way connection points are.

Let's take another look at the purchase funnel in today's world.

THE MARKETING FUNNEL

DISINGENUOUS

one-way communication

AWARENESS
CONSIDERATION
CONVERSION
LOYALTY

GENUINE

two-way participation

PERSONALIZED
PHONE CALLS

REWARDS
CLUB MEMBERSHIP
SWEEPSTAKES
PUNCH CARDS
SALES CALLS
GAMES/CONTESTS
CRM ECOM
EXPERIENTIAL
VIDEO
CO-CREATION
MEMBERSHIPS
ROBUST CLUB

IN-STORE
SOCIAL CONTENT
APPS
YOUTUBE
ONLINE CONTESTS
OPT IN
GAMIFICATION
CLICK to BUY
PUSH NOTIFICATION

COUPONS FSI'S
CONSUMER REPORTS
SALES PROMOTION
MAGAZINES
EXPERIENTIAL/EVENTS
DIRECT MAIL
TELEMARKETING
RE-MESSAGING
WEBSITES PPC
SEARCH/SEO
QR CODES/SNAP TAGS
BLOGGER
NATIVE ADVERTISING
LINK BAIT
MOBILE COUPONING
INFLUENCERS
RE-TARGETING

TRADITIONAL
TV RADIO
PRINT
POS PR
BANNER ADS
GOOGLE ADS
SOCIAL ADS
PROGRAMMATIC

awareness ▶ consideration ▶ conversion ▶ loyalty

X

PARTICIPATION

=

MORE AWARENESS

x participation = more awareness

We saw how connectivity has been incredibly effective on the right side of the equation, yet most advertising budgets are still firmly set on the left side of this equation.

Use this chart to assess your current brand spend. Consider moving 10% at a time to the right, and create more programs that allow consumers to become part of your activations.

The C-suites will move over eventually as digital advertising has surpassed TV spend for the first time.

TV as a medium produces great content. What it doesn't produce is great engagement. That work will be done one-on-one and in the trenches.

DIGITAL ADVERTISING HAS SURPASSED TV SPEND FOR THE FIRST TIME

TV: $72 B
36%
of spend

DIGITAL: $77.5 B
38%
of spend

Source: eMarketer 2017 prediction

A NEW WAY OF THINKING
ABOUT MARKETING

The era of Marketing Warfare is done. It's time to adopt a new mindset and shift your way of thinking.

....

Here are a few new rules to guide you. Print them out. Post them by your desk. Go back to them as often as you can.

- Begin with the consumer's POV every time. Every single time.

- Build your activations and programs around your consumers (not your brand)!

- Be ready for change every day. (The market place is evolving and marketers need to keep up)!

- Give attention first. Then worry about getting it.

- Nurture your brand advocates. Word of mouth is your most powerful weapon.

THE NEW RULES FOR MARKETERS

....

begin with the
CONSUMER'S POV.

build around
YOUR CONSUMERS
(not your brand)!

be ready for
CHANGE EVERY DAY.

GIVE ATTENTION FIRST.
then worry about getting it.

nurture your
BRAND ADVOCATES.
word of mouth is your most
powerful weapon.

....

INSTEAD OF YOUR
TARGET AUDIENCE

THINK ABOUT YOUR
TARGET'S AUDIENCE

STOP THE MARKETING WARFARE

....

START PLAYING THE PARTICIPATION GAME

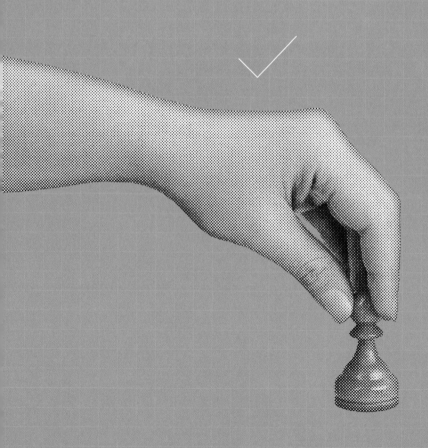

WHERE CAN YOU START?

Shifting your way of thinking—and your organization's—can be tough.

Many of the brands we work with are at different stages, and we know it's unrealistic to think you can change overnight.

We've developed a flow chart to help you take a look at what you're doing today and the way you're making decisions. The results will help you understand your biggest opportunities and direct you back to the most relevant thought starters at the end of each chapter for you.

dive in and discover where to get started ·················▸

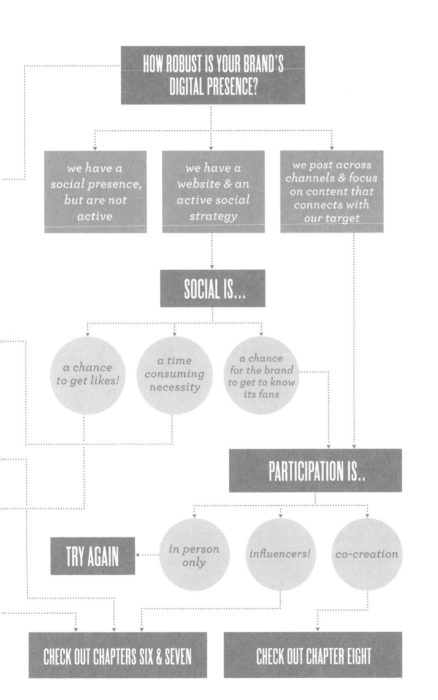

MANY THANKS TO
THE PARTICIPANTS

Our team at Moosylvania continues to uncover new ideas every day and produce Moose Tracker reports. We used a lot of their info in the context of this work and we are very grateful for their continuing efforts.

Rachel McInnis, Creative Director at Moose, provided the final touch to the writing and editing. She fills in the blanks and makes her points beautifully. She devised the game at the end and brought it to life. She also worked hand in hand with our designers and creative directed the effort.

Jillian Flores, our Director of Brand Planning, helped from the very start as we isolated 150 case studies and wove the stories into this book. She is instrumental in designing our base research every year and helping to articulate theory with examples. She worked with Rachel to create the game and bring it to life.

Lauren Knobloch, former Moose employee, was chosen to create the flow and design of the book and was incredibly artful and persistent as she read each and every word before designing the type to express it. Concept and visuals are her stock in trade, and we were excited to get her on this project.

Hilary Clements, another former Moose employee, designed the cover and did the original set up for the project. She illustrated it and worked through multiple renditions to bring it life. Her style is original and compelling and we're always thrilled to work with her.

Krista Knuffman, from Great Questions, has been instrumental for five years—helping to set up our research efforts and find the nuggets that inform our conclusions. She patiently absorbs our challenges and turns them into statistics we can use.

Thanks to Moose creative Sara Klarfeld for adding her touch to the design and production throughout the process.

Special thanks to Madeline Houston, our terrific summer intern from my alma mater, University of Missouri, School of Journalism. She did most of the research and case studies that formed the initial thesis.

The editorial team at Idea Press and editor David Moldawer, provided on-going assistance and a solid foundation. I'm thrilled to have worked with David and received his direction and assistance in telling a complete story.

My wife Lori—who just assumed I was watching sports at the office on Saturdays and Sundays while we put this together.

Norty Cohen

INDEX

REFERENCE INDEX

Wendy's Pretzel Love Songs: *Source: YouTube*
Peach Pumpkin Ale/AB Super Bowl Ad: *Source: YouTube*
Peach Pumpkin Ale: Craft Beer Alliance Video: *Source: You Tube*
T-Mobile Unlimited Texts: *Source: Google Images*
HP Ghost Wave: *Source: You Tube*
Pizza Hut/Pepsi Ad: *Source: You Tube*
Subservient Chicken: *Source: Google Images*
McDonald's Pay with Loving: *Source: You Tube*
Kate Spade Misadventures: *Source: You Tube*
Marvel Captain America: *Source: Google Images*
Say it With Pepsi: *Source: Google Images*
Mountain Dewcision: *Source: Google Images*
#Cokemyname: *Source: Google Images*
Tweet a Coke: *Source: Google Images*
Honda Dream Track: *Source: Google Images*
Starbucks Frappuccino Flavoff: *Source: Google Images*
Aeriereal: *Source: Aerireal.com*
Lay's Photo Bags: *Source: Google Images*
Wendy's Share4Adoption: *Source: Wendy's.com*
Samsung S7mypic: *Source: Google Images*
Chipotle Haiku: *Source: Google Images*
Jordan #Re2spect: *Source: Google Images*
Dr. Pepper #PickYourPepper: *Source: Google Images*
Ford Fiestagram: *Source: Google Images*
Nordstrom Study Break: *Source: Google Images*
Disney Mad Hatter: *Source: Google Images*
WalMart Greenlight A Vet: *Source: Google Images*
Amazon Prime Box: *Source: Google Images*
Apple Shot on iPhone: *Source: Google Images*
Michael Kors Watch Hunger Stop: *Source: Google Images*
Chevrolet Best Day Ever: *Source: Google Images*
Sapporo Moped: *Source: Moosylvania*
Minecraft: *Source: You Tube*
ESPN Fantasy Football App: *Source: Google Images*
Ford Escape NYC: *Source: Google Images*
BMW's Eyes on Gigi: *Source: Google Images*
Nike Vending Machine: *Source: Google Images*
JC Penney Play to Give: *Source: Google Images*
Sony Playstation Mobile Game: *Source: Google Images*
Honda Stage: *Source: You Tube*
Netflix House of Cards: *Source: You Tube*
Verizon Minecraft: *Source: Google Images*
Old Navy Never Basic: *Source: Google Images*
Nike Ky-Rispie Kreme: *Source: Google Images*
Chick-fil-A Cow Appreciation Day: *Source: Google Images*
North Face Never Stop Exploring: *Source: Google Images*
Taco Bell Emoji: *Source: Google Images*
Gap Close the Pay Gap: *Source: Google Images*
Vans Living off the Wall: *Source: Google Images*
Google Shares the Pride: *Source: Google Images*
H&M Close the Loop: *Source: Google Images*
Chase Morning Bell: *Source: Google Images*
Converse Made by You: *Source: Google Images*
Chapter imagery and support visuals: *Getty Images*
Charts and Diagrams: *Moosylvania*